The Victorian Development of the Clifton, Montpelier and Powis Estates of Brighton

Steve Myall

Front cover illustration:
Detail of St Michael and All Angels' church, Brighton
Steel engraving published by Rock & Co, London, 13 July 1866

Frontispiece:
Detail from the 1849 deeds to 2 Powis Villas.

Back cover:
Detail from Leppard's 1839 Directory (see chapters 6 and 8).

British Library Cataloguing-in-Publication Data.
A catalogue record for this book is available from the British Library.

ISBN 978-0-9559006-0-0

Published by Pomegranate Press, 51 St Nicholas Lane, Lewes, Sussex BN7 2JZ
telephone: 01273 470100; email: sussexbooks@aol.com
website: www.pomegranate-press.co.uk

Printed and bound in China.

The Victorian Development
of the Clifton, Montpelier and Powis Estates
of Brighton

Steve Myall

with additional research by
Brian Brooks and Roger Amerena

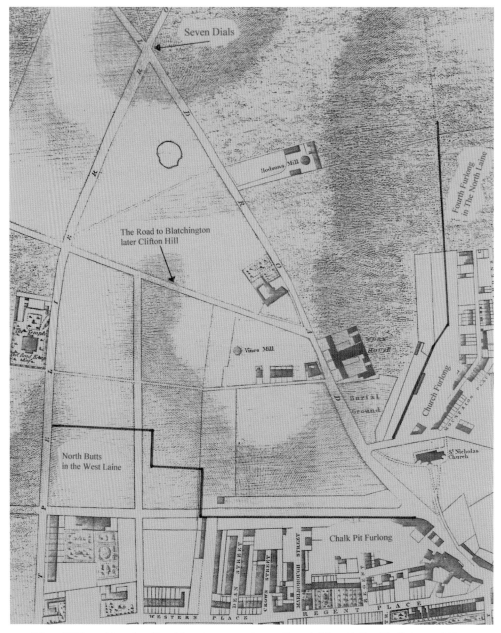

The Clifton-Montpelier-Powis area from the J.Pigott Smith 'Map of the Town of Brighton, 1824-5'.
The earlier furlong divisions have been added in red, together with the later positions of the Seven Dials and Clifton Hill.

CONTENTS:

ACKNOWLEDGEMENTS:

For the research behind this book the author offers his particular thanks to Henry Smith for his most generous and enthusiastic help and to John and Jill Ford for giving their time to read through the final draft and offer much appreciated thoughts and corrections. Among those local residents who offered the deeds to their properties for inspection, gave freely of their knowledge of the area and allowed me into their homes, grateful thanks go to Peter and Carol Woodhead, Robert Gregory, Mrs. Y. Clarke, the late H.E. Tappin, Camilla Dinkel, Mr. and Mrs. Alan Crisp, the late Louis-Francois Duchene, Dominic and Philippa Sankey, John Tyson, Philip Engleman, Jessica Rutherford, James Noble, John and Ruth, Julia and Hal Doyne-Ditmus, Shan Lancaster, Ron Martin, Dean Law, Douglas and Jill Clisby, Mick Hamer, Naomi Padmore, Zeta Latham and Louise Schweitzer.

My thanks also go to Brian Brooks for his research and patient note-taking, to Roger Amerena for his enthusiastic insistence that the book must be published, to Geoffrey Mead, Maureen Brand, Sue Berry, Roy Grant, Mary Horsfield, John Blackwell, Peter J. Hill, the late Ken Fines, Laurie Keen, Stephen Henley, Andrew Barlow, Andrew Bennett and staff at the East Sussex Record Office, and staff in the Administration Office of the Royal Alexandra Hospital for Sick Children, who all contributed their specialist knowledge or found valuable documents. Thanks also go to Martin Ross, who read and interpreted many old deeds, Mrs. Vine Molony for the colour illustration of Vine's Mill, and 'Step Back in Time' of Queens Road, who helped with illustrations of the three local churches and Arnold House, all buildings which are no longer with us.

Thanks are also given to all those who deposited documents at the ESRO, from which valuable information was gathered. The Brighton & Hove Archivist would like to respectfully request that anyone presently holding historical documents should consider depositing them at the Record Office. The Record Office does not assume ownership of the documents, but merely takes the role of safe custodian and carefully offers them for inspection to all interested parties and future generations. If you feel you would like to respond to this offer, the address is: The East Sussex Record Office,
    The Maltings, Castle Precinct,
    LEWES BN7 2YT.

Final thanks to Norah Granger, without whom this project would never have started.

1

The Early Owners of a Piece of Sheep Down

This book describes the early Victorian residential development of a piece of eighteenth century sheep down. The land is unnamed on the c1740 map of 'Brighton Parish' but by the 'Parish of Brighton 1792' map (Brighton History Centre) the particular area is identified as Church Hill – West Side, and its eastern boundary is Dyke Road, known at that time as the Road from Steyning. Its western boundary is the route that became Montpelier Road, and the two roads join to the north as the apex of the triangle of land. The southern limit on this 1792 map is something of a zig-zag, vaguely following the east-west route of what is now Upper North Street. However, the subject of this book will go south of that line, to include some streets on the sea-ward side of Western Road, which are very much a part of the Montpelier district. It is also necessary to take a step to the east of our Dyke Road boundary to look at the oldest building on Church Hill, St. Nicholas' Church, and the largest on the Hill, Brighton's second Workhouse, erected just north of the church in 1821. Finally, the Wick Estate and the Chalybeate Spring are included, as the western neighbours to Thomas Read Kemp's Temple residence on Montpelier Road.

While it is convenient to divide the area into the three names of Clifton, Montpelier and Powis, as a whole this side of Church Hill holds a unique place in Brighton's Victorian history. As the story unfolds, it becomes evident that the area is the first in Brighton to represent the newly emerging influences and architectural aspirations of the middle classes in the town. This was partly through the entrepreneurial spirit of an influential Welshman, and partly through the new confidence of the increasingly affluent business and professional classes working side by side with the many local builders and craftsmen in the town – builders who also saw their earnings and social position improved with Brighton's Victorian property boom. The final happy coincidence with these influences was the career of Amon Henry Wilds. In addition the story reviews one of the several paintings of our area by John Constable before the builders moved in; there is a contemporary illustration of the first house built on Clifton Hill (illustrated on the back cover), and a glimpse of the Temple Fields Cricket

Ground where Montpelier Crescent now stands, together with details of a local vicarage owned by the canon of a cathedral church in Canada. Church Hill is also viewed within the wider town's development, and the book looks at important contemporary events in Brighton while the area is being built. This triangle of land covers about half of the Church Hill sheep down: the other half is east of the Road from Steyning. This half is also named Church Hill on the 1792 map, but without the 'West Side' distinction, and its eastern boundary is a line just to the east of the northerly continuation of the present St. Nicholas Road. These two sides of Church Hill were measured out in acres, rods and pauls for the purpose of defining ownership, but they were never included in the laine and furlong agricultural divisions of the town, and the eastern and southern boundaries may tell us why. On the 1792 map the eastern limit of the Church Hill sheep down, beside the present St. Nicholas Road, seems to be defined by how far up the slope of the hill the tenant farmers of North Laine can reasonably work their land. When it becomes too steep the North Laine series of pauls and furlongs stops, and the sheep down begins. On the southern end of Church Hill – West Side this difficulty of farming on the slopes is even more clearly illustrated. On the hillside nearest Dyke Road and St. Nicholas' Church, the steepest part, Chalk Pit Furlong in West Laine stretches only a little way up Church Hill. As the tenant farmers went westwards, past where the present Windmill Pub is, the slope of the hill lessens and the paul-pieces of Hedge Furlong and North Butts make much greater inroads onto Church Hill – West Side.

So the area may have been partly defined by hillside farming limitations. Sheep grazed on Church Hill, and neither east nor west of the Road from Steyning ever became part of the famous Brighthelmstone agricultural laines that surrounded the old town. Indeed it was among these sheep and their shepherds that the water of the mineral spring, later named St. Ann's Well, first made its name, before Dr. Russell found it. As Musgrave (1981) wrote, 'The waters of the well had some reputation for promoting fruitfulness, local shepherds having observed the remarkable fecundity of the sheep that drank from it'.

The land's early ownership can be traced through the Danish King Canute (d1035), who gave the title of Earl of the West Saxons to Godwin (d1052), together with manors in Sussex, including Brighthelmstone and Rottingdean (Berry 2005). Godwin was an important landowner in England, and although an Anglo-Saxon he gave his support to Canute when the Dane became King in 1016. Today Godwin is viewed, after the monarch, as probably the most powerful man in England under four successive kings. Godwin's eldest son, Harold, succeeded to these Sussex manors, later being chosen as King on the death of Edward the Confessor in 1065, only to lose his life a year later at Hastings. By the 1792 map our tract of arable land had two owners. On Church

Hill – West Side Thomas Kemp (1745–1811, Thomas Read Kemp's father) is listed as owning 41 acres, 2 rods and 38 pauls, with the 3rd Duke of Dorset listed as owning 5 acres, 3 rods and 34 pauls. These two families also owned the land on the east side of the hill. This Dorset was our ambassador to France when the revolution broke in 1789. In the previous generation the 2nd Earl of Thanet, John Tufton, married Margaret the eldest daughter of Richard, Earl of Dorset, and the youngest of their four sons, Colonel Sackville Tufton, inherited the moiety of Brighton – Lewes some time before 1706. His son, the 7th Earl of Dorset, sold his share of the title to Thomas Friend of Brighton in 1737. Thomas Friend became Lord of the Manor jointly with Mrs. Elizabeth Sparrow (Salzman 1940). The land of the Manor was apportioned between Friend and the widow of John Sparrow by a Chancery Order in May 1761 (ESRO AMS6167/1/1-9). Regarding these old land measurements, a paul was a long, narrow, cultivated strip, usually about one eighth of an acre. Sawyer (1881) describes the land area of 'Laines' as being peculiar to the parishes in and around Brighton, as far as Lewes, and then adds, 'the term "paul" cannot be traced to any other parish in the county except Brighton'.

John and Sue Farrant (1978) produced a list of 'Owners of Pieces in the Common Laines' in the Brighton area in 1739. They note the reduction in the number of individual holdings between 1700 and 1780, which consolidation was mainly due to the activities of two families, Friend/Kemp and Masters/Tidy. Richard Masters, baptised in Brighton in 1680, appears to be the first person with a clear policy of land acquisition in and around the town, but it is the Friend/Kemp family which is involved in our area. The land holdings of the Friend family date back before 1584, at which date John Friend and nineteen other inhabitants purchased the ruined Priory together with land and buildings 'commonly called the Bartholomews' (Robinson 1967). Erredge (1862) tells the same story of the sale of this property but records it as 'Thomas Friend and others . . . in consideration of the sum of £44'. By 1739 John Friend from Portslade and Thomas Friend of Brighton, both have interests in the town. As mentioned, the purchases of Thomas Friend, which started in 1737, were more ambitious than Masters'. Dale (1967) describes Thomas Friend as owning a great deal of land in Lewes, Brighton and the neighbourhood, including the copyhold tenure of Lewes Castle, Barbican House and a full moiety (often a half portion) of the Manor of Brighton. He died in 1762, and in his will dated 6th March 1761 (quoted in the deeds to 14 Sillwood Road – chapter 10) his land holdings passed to his nephew, also called Thomas Friend. This second Thomas Friend died just a year later, on 23rd December 1763. His nephew John Bull gained the inheritance but sold it in 1770 to his cousin John Kemp, a nephew to the first Thomas Friend. John Kemp died without issue on 29th September 1774 and the land passed to his nephew Thomas Kemp, who finally passed it to his son, Thomas Read Kemp. It was during his ownership that the development of our area began. The fact of two earlier owners being called Thomas Friend and dying within a year of each other has caused some confusion in several history books of the town. However, the two lines of the family are explained in Salzman's 'Victoria History of the County of Sussex' (1940), and the dates of both these gentlemen are confirmed in the deeds to 14 Sillwood Road, which describe the title of Ann Sober (née Kemp) to her home, Western Lodge, and its surrounding gardens. Thomas and Anne (née Read) Kemp had five children of whom two survived: Ann (later Mrs. Sober) born in 1775, and Thomas Read, born in Lewes in 1782. The continuation of Dorset as an owner on the early maps, and again in the nineteenth century, is explained by a deed in the East Sussex Record Office. On 17th and 18th January 1805, these two children of Thomas Kemp sold part of the land on Church Hill to Arabella Diana (Sackville), Duchess of Dorset, and her husband Charles, Earl Whitworth (ESRO AMS 6382). The Sackville family's interest in the area stems from the ancient 11th century title for the lordship of Brightelstan Michelham, which was first held by Earl Godwin, the original owner mentioned earlier. Earl Godwin's title passed through Henry VIII and Elizabeth I, before coming to Thomas Sackville, born at Buckhurst, Sussex, c1530 and created 1st Earl of Dorset in 1604. His descendant, Lionel Cranfield Sackville, the 7th Earl, was created Duke of Dorset in 1720. The Dorset titles became extinct with the death of the 5th Duke, Charles Sackville-Germain, in 1843, and the family sold the title for Brightelstan Michelham, now referred to as 'The Lordship of Brighton', in 1988. It was then won in a newspaper competition by Jackie Aistrup, a London secretary, who later sold it by auction at the Historical Records Agency on May 30th 1996. The title was bought by an anonymous bidder, thought to be the boxing champion Chris Eubank, for £45,000.

On 19th and 20th November 1817 the Sackville family sold this same property back to Thomas Read Kemp and his uncle and trustee, Nathaniel Kemp of Ovingdean, for £1,610. In the deeds the property is described as a piece of sheep down, 20 acres, 3 rods and 22 pauls, on the west side of Brighton, and while the Sackville family owned it the arable area had been divided into two fields which were occupied and farmed by Kemp and William Acton (ESRO AMS 6382). (See explanation of 'Ovington near Brighton' print in chapter 11). Acton's name also appears in the records from the Children's Hospital, and by 1845 he lived at 6 Wykeham Terrace, renting the house from George Lowdle who owned and rented out the whole terrace (ESRO BH/B/4/36b/2). This 1817 deed also puts some names to the ownership of this part of the Downs prior to Thomas Friend's buying policy. The family names mentioned are the Earl of the Isle of Thanet, who married into the inheritance through the Dorset family, then the names of Shadwell, Gunn, William Vinall,

Charles Callis Western and his close relative Thomas Western. This is the family that gave its name to Western Road which runs across the southern end of our area. Charles Callis Western (1767–1844), owner of further land on Church Hill, had inherited the Rivenhall Estate in Essex on his coming of age in 1788. He became the Rt. Hon. Charles Callis Baron Western of Rivenhall, MP for Maldon, Essex. His parliamentary life started in 1789 and continued uninterrupted for 42 years. He was very highly thought of as a social reformer, a protector of those who worked on the land and an 'enlightened statesman'. His headstone at Rivenhall Church reads, 'Lord and Baron of Essex'. Among the untitled hand-written Sussex Pamphlets 120 (2) in the Brighton History Centre, Masters, Friend and Gunn are described as 'descendants of the aboriginies (sic) of the town'.

On 12th July 1806 Thomas Read Kemp married Frances, the fourth daughter of Sir Francis Baring, Bart., at Beddington in Surrey. Sir Francis, with his brother John, had founded Baring Brothers Bank and was chairman of the East India Company in 1792/93. In 1807 Thomas Kemp senior purchased Herstmonceux Place for the young couple. Kemp purchased the estate from Francis Hare, grandson of the Bishop of Chichester, who had gained Herstmonceux Castle by his marriage to Bethaia Naylor, around 1727. Kemp senior died on 3rd May 1811, and after settling a £10,000 trust on his daughter, the rest of his very considerable estate he left to his son Thomas Read. Musgrave (1981) tells us that Thomas Read Kemp lived the rich social life that accompanied such wealth, but probably under the influence of his wife's sister, an enthusiastic evangelical Christian, gave up his seat in Parliament and became the minister of a dissenting Christian congregation, for which he built a chapel in Lewes, and one in Ship Street, Brighton. In 1819 he sold Herstmonceux Place, together with the ruined castle, and on land he now owned in Brighton had a large mansion built, the Temple, now the Brighton & Hove High School in Montpelier Road. Kemp, of course, had a wide choice of sites for his new Brighton home. But rather than taking a hilltop view over the town, a fair proportion of which he owned, or building to the east near his uncle and trustee, he went west, out of the town and out of view behind Church Hill. His reasons may be explained partly by a wish to be away from the social whirl of the centre of town, but also by an article in the *Brighton Gazette*, June 17th 1824, recommending the Chalybeate, (now St. Ann's Well Gardens) the curative mineral spring beside Kemp's chosen site:

'Surrounded on the northern and western sides by a plantation of firs, and open on the east and south, (this area) commands a beautiful view of cornfields, meadows etc., to the ocean, and is unquestionably one of the most pleasant and rural situations in the vicinity of Brighton'.

It was certainly a lovely area for Kemp to build his Temple, and the famous Chalybeate waters nearby, which a few years later became a favourite venue of Queen Adelaide, were claimed to cure most ailments. Martin (1871) also writes that in the early nineteenth century 'Rustic Fetes and Public Breakfasts were much in vogue in fashionable society, and one of the principal places of rendezvous was the Chalybeate and grounds on the Wick Estate'.

It was Dr. Richard Russell, said to be the founder of fashionable Brighton, who in addition to his medical recommendation of sea-water, 'discovered' the chalybeate spring, making use of it for treating patients. Dr. Russell died in 1759, but the spring was known before his recommendation and already had a reputation locally, apart from among the shepherds and their sheep mentioned earlier.

Watercolour of the Chalybeate, c.1795, inscribed top right 'At Wick, near Brighton, Sussex' and depicting the 'plantation of firs' described in the Brighton Gazette article.

Russell's clientele included the powerful and influential Pelham and Gage families, and he gathered such a following that he built himself a permanent home in Brighton, the present site of the Royal Albion Hotel, Old Steine. At the Chalybeate, Russell erected a temporary structure over the spring (illustrated above), which was later replaced by a small classical edifice (illustrated in chapter 5), and this in turn was demolished by Hove Corporation in 1934 (Dale 1972). By 1800, some 41 years after Dr. Russell died, an annual subscription for taking the waters for a season was 10s 6d, and non-subscribers paid 6d for a bottle.

It was Sir Isaac Lyon Goldsmid (1778–1859) the financier and Jewish communal leader, who laid out the six acres of St. Ann's Well Gardens that we know today, in 1850. In the mid 1890s they were used for filming by George Albert Smith, the early cinema pioneer. Musgrave (1981) writes that Smith's first cinema studio in St. Ann's Well Gardens was thought to have been the earliest of its kind in the world. By 1900 Smith leased and managed what was then described as 'St. Ann's Well and Wild Garden', (Robertson's *Brighton & Hove*, 1901). In his advertisement Smith lists the amusements as 'Lawn Tennis, Ices and light refreshments, free swings, free monkey house, the "Famous Iron Water" – free, boat swings, shooting, cocoa-nuts and glass houses selling ferns, flowers, cucumbers and grapes.' Weekday admission was 3d and Sundays was 6d. In an earlier generation Amon Henry Wilds had often won prizes in archery competitions held on the Wick Estate.

At the site marking the location of the spring today is an inscription telling us that the lover of the Anglo-Saxon Lady Anne Frida was murdered near the site, and her tears were said to be the original source of the spring waters. On official notices in and around the park the name of 'Ann' is variously spelt with or without the final 'e'.

Regarding Goldsmid as a Jewish leader in the town, although the Jewish community was only small in Brighton in the mid-nineteenth century, the town was in the unique position of having Henry Solomon as its chief constable. His brother-in-law, Hyam Lewis was a town commissioner and member of the first police committee, and a second brother-in-law, Levy Emmanuel Cohen, was an early proprietor of the *Brighton Guardian*. Hyam's son, Benjamin Lewis, was also a town commissioner and all were active in the affairs of the synagogue in Devonshire Place (Spector – unpublished manuscript – Brighton History Centre).

Solomon himself was a watchmaker before entering service for the town commissioners in 1821, but came to an untimely death in 1844 at the hands of a petty thief he was questioning in the police office at the town hall. Such was the esteem with which he was held in the town that a subscription of over £1,000 was raised for his widow and nine children (d'Enno 2007).

In the 1822 Directories by Baxter and T.H. Boore, named in the list of local commissioners, are Nathaniel Kemp of Ovingdean Hall, and T.R. Kemp of 'Brighton Mansion' which, along with 'Kemp's Folly', was an early name for the Temple. In neither of these early 1820 directories is Montpelier Road mentioned. Nathaniel Kemp was a very influential figure in the town. By 1833, among other positions, he was a trustee of the Female Orphan Asylum in Gloucester Street, and on the committee of the Brighton Dispensary in Middle Street. His wife was one of the founders of the National Schools, and one of the schools' lovely buildings was the Gothic edifice at the bottom of Church Street. Nathaniel Kemp's home is now Ovingdean Hall School for children with hearing impairments, and has the style of a very attractive but smaller version of Stanmer House.

'Swiss Cottage, Chalybeate.' Lithograph published by Mason and Ackermann, c1835.
This stood at the entrance to the Chalybeate grounds, where visitors would leave their
servants and horses. In Saunders' 1837 Directory visitors to Brighton were told
'A Commodious and elegant building, (seen middle distance to the right, also illustrated
in chapter 5) comprising a reading room and other conveniences, has been recently
erected, together with a pretty rustic cottage'.

Thomas Read Kemp's first wife, Frances Baring, died in 1825 after the birth of her tenth child, and he married the widowed Frances Margaretta Harvey on 26th November 1832 at All Souls, Marylebone. During this first quarter of the nineteenth century, before Thomas Read and the first Mrs. Kemp had made their home on the far side of Church Hill, there was already an established and eccentric resident on the near side of the hill, just below the church. Erredge (1862) writes that in 1809 there is an entry in the vestry book:-

'Oct 2nd 1809 that Corporal Staines be allowed a blanket and a great coat during the winter.'

This Corp. Staines was an old marine who had served under Nelson at the Siege of Copenhagen in 1801. He was very crippled and made a living by making miniature chalk soldiers, cannons and fortifications. On great national anniversaries it was his custom to fire royal salutes from four pistol barrels that he had formed into a battery. Corp. Staines' first home in Brighton was a cave hewn into the chalk in the side of the Church Hill chalk pit, which was at the eastern end of what is now Upper North Street, just across the road from St. Nicholas' Church. As such, he was one of only three residents of Church Hill at this time. He then moved from the chalk pit into a hut he built for himself, east of the Manor Pound at the back of St. Nicholas'. Possibly when the Workhouse was built, he moved again to the Round Hill area, but later returned to Church Hill, eventually dying in the Workhouse, with his last wish being that he was buried close to Phoebe Hessel, (Martin 1871). If he was in residence at the time, no doubt the corporal would have been amused by the sham battle that was enacted on Church Hill on September 25th 1803, to practise repelling an expected invasion force. Unfortunately the townsfolk heard about this exercise the night before, and on the morning of these military manoeuvres much of Brighton's population came up the hill to watch – chaos ensued! Roy Grant adds that the event became known as 'The Battle of Church Hill', and the regiments involved were the militia of the South Gloucesters, the Sussex Volunteers, the South Hampshires and the regular troops of the Flying Artillery. For nearly a decade into the 1800s, after England's declaration of war with France in 1793, the large military presence in Brighton meant parades, grand reviews, field-days and sham fights. The intention was always to keep the strictest military discipline, but the townsfolk viewed them as entertainment.

Corporal Staines, in front of his Manor Pound hut, just north of St. Nicholas' Church. Aquatint engraving by C.A. Epps, published c1820 in J. Whittemore's children's book 'Harry and Lucy's Trip to Brighton'. The book was written by the children's mother and is described as 'a humorous and picturesque description of the amusements and scenery of this fashionable watering place'.

In chapter 8 the Marchant map of 1808 is illustrated, with no sign of Montpelier Road. He published another map of the town in 1815, again with no Montpelier Road, but both these maps have 'the Carriage Road' that became Clifton Hill, and the footpath that became Vine Place and Victoria Road. So both these east-west routes pre-date the establishing of the north-south roadway that became Montpelier Road. Kemp had the Temple built by 1819, so Montpelier Road was probably established as a carriage-way sometime between 1815 and 1819, and probably nearer to 1819 as it is not mentioned in the 1820 Brighton Directories. On the final map in this chapter, dated 1822,

Montpelier Road has no northerly extension beyond its junction with what became Clifton Hill. Indeed, beyond that junction there was nowhere for it to go other than join up with the Steyning/Henfield Road. All this suggests that Kemp's Temple was the origin of Montpelier Road. It served as the route from his new home down to the sea front. Its northern extension up to the junction with what became Clifton Hill was a logical step, enabling Kemp to drive a carriage to the Chalybeate to the west, or St. Nicholas' to the east.

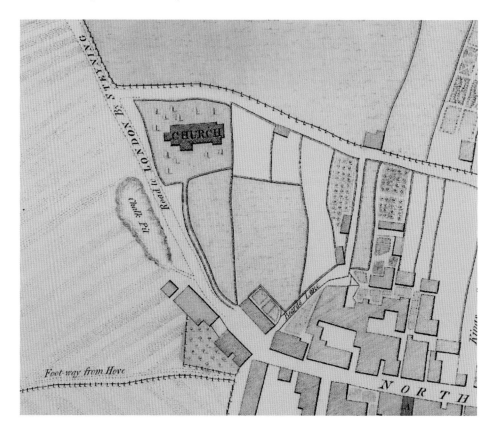

The above detail of 'The New and Correct Plan of Brighthelmstone' was published by Thomas Budgen in 1788. It shows the chalk pit that became Corp. Staines' home just south of the church. The small footway that leads into the chalk pit, turning off the Road to London by Steyning, is the junction that became the turning into Upper North Street. At the base of the map the 'Foot way from Hove' is the route that became Western Road. In 1788, travelling westwards up North Street, there was a left, then right, kink in the road to get onto the foot way to Hove, and that movement in the road is still there today, as North Street turns into Western Road, just past the Clock Tower.

The following map by W. Belch, dated 1822 but published in Baxter's 'Stranger in Brighton' of 1824, shows the Temple, with the pathway to the Chalybeate that became Victoria Road, and just above that is the carriage-way that became the Road to Blatchington, later Clifton Hill. Also seen are Vine's Mill with his cottage, and the newly built Workhouse. The long rectangle just across the Road to Blatchington from Vine's Mill is either the soap manufactory of Mr. Heard or the beginnings of the Church Hill School, which was started the year of this map. The mill to the north is Hodson's. The Road to Blatchington is the most northerly east-west route. However at this time its destination was only the Chalybeate Spring, so the name of 'Blatchington' was not attached to it until its westerly route was extended a few years later. On this map, Corp. Staines' chalk pit looks as if it has some development on it, and this was, or most likely became, the Chalk Pit Island tenements listed in the Rate Book mentioned in chapter 6. There is another developed chalk pit shown, north and to the west of the church, with other developments directly to the east. These would have been the Mount Zion Place tenements mentioned in the next chapter, but they were probably not quite as extensive as this map suggests. This map also highlights three large mansion homes which feature in the early development of the southern limits of our area.

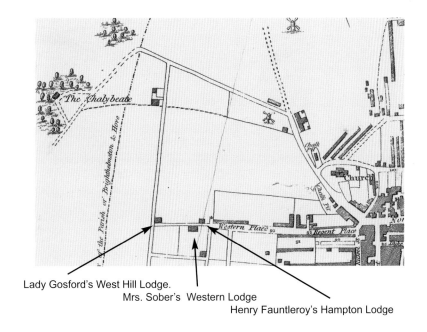

Lady Gosford's West Hill Lodge.
Mrs. Sober's Western Lodge
Henry Fauntleroy's Hampton Lodge

2

Thomas Read Kemp Sells Church Hill – West Side

T.R. Kemp lived with his first wife at the Temple, on the western boundary of the particular area that is the subject of this book, and it is worthwhile looking at Kemp's ownership and title to the land of Clifton, Montpelier and Powis. A local historian has some notes on the Powis district of Brighton supplied to him by the late Mr.J.S. Gray (undated), the owner of a famous Brighton photographic collection currently held at the Royal Pavilion. These notes seem to represent personal recollection of the history, and in them Gray writes:

'Powis Grove, Road, Square and Villas stand on three and one half acres of land purchased in 1846 by John Yearsley for £1,100. He was a partner in the firm of Williams and Yearsley, ironmongers of North Street, and was a native of Powysland in Wales. In consequence he gave the name of Powis to the streets which were laid out on his land.'

Two local deeds establish that Gray has made a simple mistake over the nature of the deal and the price, but his introduction of an important developer, Mr. Yearsley from Welshpool, is an accurate and valuable reference.

Moore (c1970), in her article 'Three Brighton Streets', includes an extract from a codicil to Thomas Read Kemp's will, dated 21st September 1835, in which Kemp specifies an area of land in the West Laine being left to his son. Moore does not try to identify this land, but assumes it 'must have lain immediately to the north of our area': immediately to the north of Moore's three streets are the Powis and Clifton estates. Remembering Gray's description of the three and one half acres which he says Yearsley purchased and developed into the Powis estate, it is clear that the land Kemp specifically left to his eldest son, Thomas Nathaniel, was that which became the Clifton and Powis estates. To quote from the will:

'. . . and all that piece of land . . in the west laine . . by estimation three acres and a half, bounded on the north by a road leading to Blatchington,' (the present Clifton Hill points directly at Blatchington mill and is called 'the Road to Blatchington' on early maps), 'on the west by the Montpelier Road, on the south by another road leading to the workhouse,' (this is Vine Place, most of which is now called Victoria Road, and leads straight to the old workhouse site from Montpelier Road) 'and on the east by another road leading from the said last' (Vine Place) 'to the said first mentioned road' (this first mentioned road being Clifton Hill).

This last boundary road on the east is Dyke Road (previously named as the Road from Steyning, but by now called the Road from Henfield), which does indeed join Vine Place with Clifton Hill on the eastern side of the area in question. This piece of land lies directly to the east of Kemp's Temple home and describes the Clifton/Powis section of our area.

Further proof of Kemp's continued ownership at this time came with the locating of local house deeds. For example, 14 Victoria Road, built in 1838, has the deed of purchase for the land on which numbers 14 and 15 stand. The deed is dated 24th November 1834, between T.R. Kemp the vendor and two builders, Robert Ackerson and Thomas Pelling. The site was 73 feet by 68 feet, for which they paid Kemp £205. This of course means that Gray's suggestion of Yearsley buying the three and a half acres as bounded by particular roads, must take into account those parcels of land that Kemp had already sold off. Presumably Gray's statement of acreage is a quote from Kemp's will, and Kemp's words are 'by estimation three acres and a half'. The piece of land as bounded by the four roads described in the will is actually nearer four and a half acres. A difficulty also arises because, apart from those parcels already sold by Kemp and built on, as in Victoria Road, it is not known whether all the land covered by Vine's Mill, Mr. Vine's own house and the mill workers' cottages in Vine Place was owned by Vine or just leased by him, but taking these plots out of the equation would certainly reduce the land to nearer the three and a half acres of the will. However, the first correction to be made to Gray's recollections is the area of land that Yearsley finally purchased from Mrs. Kemp. Gray refers to these three and a half acres, which area he probably understood from Kemp's will. But a Powis Square deed tells us the land in the deal was actually 2 acres and 37 perches. So Yearsley's land purchase extended westwards to include Powis Road, but ended at the land for St. Michael's Place, which was owned by William Trocke when its development started in 1868. This area had been in his ownership for a sufficient length of time for it to become known as 'Trocke's Field' (see chapter 6,) so presumably he purchased this strip of land, between Powis Road and Montpelier Road, from Mrs. Kemp at much the same time as the Yearsley deal. Trocke was the brother of the incumbent clergyman at the Chapel Royal, the Rev. Thomas Trocke, who was responsible for the Chapel's ministry to the poor of Brighton in the early Victorian period.

The title deeds to 2 Powis Villas and 19 Powis Square, both in private collections, make more corrections to Gray's information. They tell us that the widow Frances Margaretta Kemp and her trustees (brothers of the first Mrs. Kemp) the Rt. Hon. William Baring, Henry Baring, Sir Thomas Baring (the new Baronet), Francis Thornhill Baring and Alexander Baring, Lord Ashburton, granted a lease on the land now covered by Powis Villas and the Square on 17th September 1846 (the year that Gray mentions). As Gray rightly says, the purchaser was John Yearsley, ironmonger of Brighton, but Gray implies that he bought the freehold, whereas in fact the Powis Square deeds tell us he purchased a ninety year lease, at a 'yearly rent of £105 payable half yearly on 29th September and 25th March in every year', and that he had to 'keep all buildings erected on the land in good and substantial repair'. The deeds establish that Yearsley worked in partnership with Henry Faithfull, a gentleman solicitor of Brighton and William Yearsley, solicitor of Welshpool. Henry Faithfull's brother George, who became one of Brighton's first MPs in 1833, and was one of the Brighton town commissioners, signed the lease agreement as one of the witnesses.

In the Powis Square deeds the terms of Yearley's lease are further explained. Upon prompt payment of the half yearly rent, 'if John Yearsley desires to purchase the land freehold, any time between 25th March 1849 and 25th March 1853, he should pay Mrs. Kemp £2,100'. So the personal recollection of £1,100 from Mr. J.S.Gray is also corrected. Yearsley obviously bought the freehold fairly early on in the option period, and the deeds for 2 Powis Villas confirm the house and land sale, stating that Yearsley and Faithfull of Brighton, and William Yearsley, solicitor of Welshpool, sold the land to Edward Sharp of Brighton, draper, and his trustee Arthur William Woods of Brighton, solicitor, for £480 on 30th October 1849. A house had already been built on the plot by Sharp, and the area has the strange description of "land on Church Hill round the Brig in Brighton" (this phrase can be seen at the bottom left of the frontispiece page). Also shown on this deed is an elevation with which any house in Powis Place (now Square) was to conform (next illustration). The deed also states that the houses in Powis Square were to have a building cost of at least £400 and were to enjoy the open area in the centre of the Square. Such covenants ensuring a particular standard of residential development were fairly common. The 19 Powis Square deeds indicate the 'releasing and appointment' of the plot by Yearsley and partners to John Fabian, builder, and Charles Cooper, gentleman on 7th December 1847, before Yearsley owned the freehold. There is reference to 'the intended road to be called Powis Place' and the requirement to 'share expenses of laying out and planting and keeping said lawn and pleasure ground in good order and condition'. The distance of five feet from the public way to the front of the house is also established. However, it appears that this transaction with Fabian did not result in any building work, and the leasehold was returned to Yearsley. The next deed is dated 7th June 1853 in which the Yearsley team have sold the freehold of the plot to Stephen Davey, builder, and William Parker, cement manufacturer of Shoreham. Davey had already built the house. The land was sold for £156. 15. 0d and Parker bought the new house from Davey for £693. 5. 0d. The total price of £850 indicates quite an expensive house, well above the minimum cost requirement and considerably more than the detached house of 2 Powis Villas. In chapter 8 the names of Yearsley and Davey appear again, in relation to dealings in Montpelier Street, where Davey acted as Yearsley's mortgage lender. Davey appears to be a local builder with useful resources behind him. To refer these prices to more modern times, Robert Twigger of the Economics Policy and Statistics Section of the House of Commons has estimated a multiple of 55 to equate £1 in 1830 to the year 1998, so the total sale price to Davey for house and land in Powis Square was around £47,000 in 1998 values.

A deed of 7th December 1847 also settled other leased land on William Pryce Yearsley. William Yearsley was John Yearsley's brother and William Pryce Yearsley was William Yearsley's son. Both were partners in the Welshpool firm of solicitors Howell, Jones and Yearsley. These deeds to number 2 Powis Villas illustrate some changes to the street names – for example 'Upper Powis Place' is mentioned. On early maps our present Powis Square was indeed called Powis Place, although without the 'Upper'. Powis Place – 1848 is the first mention of 'Powis' in the directories, and Sharp was the first named resident.

In the 1852 Folthorp Directory seven residents are listed in Powis Square. The entry then reads, '14 other houses unoccupied or in part unfinished'. This covers the time when Davey was building number 19, so it is likely that he was building others too. The other possibility is that, with the previous successful as-sociation between Davey and Yearsley, Stephen Davey was the builder of all the facades in Powis Square, as well as some of the complete houses. The same directory has eight residents listed in Powis Villas. Today it can be seen that all the houses in the Square conform to the 1849 deed illustration in their main features, except perhaps that the houses are bow-fronted and the drawing seems to describe the original concept as flat-fronted. Musgrave (1981) describes some of the architectural details of the houses as being 'of the early Victorian Palladian revival'. But they were not the first houses in the area to look like this, being copies of one of Wilds and Busby's original designs in Brunswick Square nearly thirty years earlier. The Powis Square homes have two fewer floors, and are a little less decorated than the Brunswick original. In chapter 3, the engraving of Christ Church also shows that the terraces of Montpelier Road, just south of Western Road, were of a similar design.

As a point of interest in the building practices of the time, a local resident reported that when replacing the basement floor in his house in Clifton Terrace, he found the original builders had dug down into the chalk and put the brickwork of the house straight onto the flat chalk bed. There were no specific foundations or preparations put in place first. This would have been the case with most of the nineteenth century houses in the town. While concrete was available in the 1850s, it was expensive and unnecessary while builders were using traditional lime mortar for the brickwork. Lime mortar is flexible, and as the moisture content of the chalk, and therefore the brickwork, varied, the walls could move without cracking. The later cement mortar is far more rigid and unforgiving.

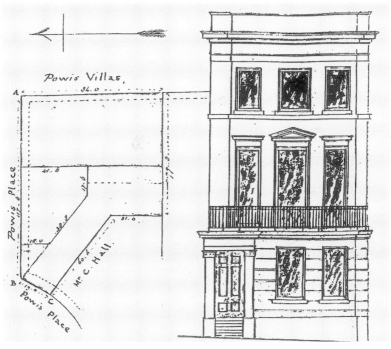

Illustration from the 2 Powis Villas deeds of 1849, showing the design to which the facades in Powis Square had to adhere.

As in Kemp Town, buyers purchased just the façade and shell, and then created their own interiors. This explains the difference in design and quality of the interiors of these homes. In these deeds the Square is identified by its first name, Powis Place. The entry of 'Mr. C. Hall' on this drawing confirms that Yearsley had already started selling off plots for houses in the square by this date.

Further deeds briefly follow the history of 2 Powis Villas. Edward Sharp of Madeira Villa, Addiscombe Road, Croydon in Surrey, gentleman, sold this house to Henry Gould Sharp of Tunbridge Wells, Kent, gentleman for £1,200 on 15th October 1869. Then on 24th March 1883 H.G.Sharp of 21 Threadneedle Street in London, gentleman, sold the house to Susannah Chapman of 11 Clifton Road, Brighton, spinster, for £1,400. The sale of small parcels of land within the near three acres left to his son (for example the two plots in Victoria Road) are indicative of the difficult times Kemp was experiencing. By 1828 he had built most of the facades to his Kemp Town development but had sold very few. On 13th November 1832 Kemp mortgaged part of the Church Hill – West Side area to the executors of Thomas Budgen, to secure a debt of £3,000. These executors were Mary Budgen, widow, Thomas Budgen of Frant, presumably the son, and Ninian (also spelt Ninyon and Nenyon in the document) Masters Bradford, gentleman of Brighton (ESRO AMS 6382). Budgen senior was a builder who had also rented a brickyard at Wick from 1808 to 1811, lived in Middle Street by the 1820s, and is thought to have died in 1826 (Beswick 1993). Erredge (1862) records that it was this Thomas Budgen who 'measured and set out in the year 1792 the terrier (from the words 'terra' and 'territory') to the tenantry land in the parish of Brighthelmstone, at present used in defining property in the parish'.

'Brunswick Square and Terrace'   Steel engraving by J. Sands after W.H. Bartlett.
Published in 1837 by Joseph Robins, London. One of the house designs at the northern end gave the inspiration for Powis Square some fifteen years after Wilds and Busby had died.

 The above illustration shows the northern side of Powis Square in 2006, where every detail of the drawing on the 1849 deed is followed. The following photographs illustrate how the design for Powis Square was taken straight from Wilds and Busby's mid 1820s model for some of the homes in Brunswick Square, top left picture, and filtered its way through the Montpelier area before making its final appearance in Powis.

Brunswick Square
Amon Wilds and
Charles Busby

Brunswick Place

Belvedere Terrace

Montpelier Road, south

Montpelier Road, north

Montpelier Place

The Brunswick Square examples can be seen in the final nine homes either side of the northern end. The front of the ground floor is flat fronted, whereas the later examples follow the curve of the upper floors, and the pediments atop the three first floor windows of the Brunswick Square homes are later confined to just the central window. So this façade can be seen percolating through various short terraces in the area before it arrives in Powis in the early 1850s, and maybe it was Stephen Davey who drew the design for the Powis Square houses on the deeds for 2 Powis Villas.

A decade before the selling of Church Hill to Yearsley, Thomas Read Kemp's finances were in ruins. So with mounting debts he moved with his family to France in 1837 and died there on December 20th 1844. He is buried at the Cemetiere du Pere-Lachaise, in the company of Edith Piaf, Oscar Wilde, Rossini, Bizet and Chopin. His epitaph simply reads, 'He sleeps in Jesus'. Hitchin-Kemp (1902) records that his death was announced as 'sudden' and suggests it may have been suicide. Two years before there was an attempt to salvage something from the ruins by a public auction on 17th and 18th January 1842, at the Old Ship Hotel. This auction was organized by George Faithfull and held by Mr. George Robins. It was advertised in the *Brighton Gazette* in 1842 and it included the Temple, described as being designed by the Wilds father and son team, and quoted as costing over £15,000 to build, also nine mansions in Kemp Town, and many let residential properties, shops and livery stables throughout the town. In addition there were several farms, Brighton racecourse and 'all the uncovered freehold land of the whole parish of Brighton', which would have included the Powis estate. The auction was a failure, and from the deeds to 3 Powis Villas it would appear that if our piece of land was included it did not sell, as indeed the Temple did not, and that while the land was left to his son as the will stated 'free from all encumbrances, which are to be discharged from his other estates', it was of course retained by his widow, Frances Margaretta.

Clifton Terrace is just the wrong side of Vine Place to be included in the Yearsley purchase, but the deeds to 1 Clifton Terrace begin to tell the story of the neighbouring development. Numbers 1 and 2 were built in 1846, the year of Yearsley's original lease agreement, and the deeds to number 1 confirm the widow Kemp's continuing interest in this area. The land for this corner house, together with number 2, was purchased by two builders, G.W. Sawyer, and Richard Edwards: Edwards then lived in the house they built. Before the Clifton Terrace house was finished, Edwards lived at 68 Upper North Street where he is listed as a surveyor. Numbers 1 and 2 were probably not the first houses to be built in the Terrace. Kelly's 1846 Directory has the first mention of Clifton Terrace, but with only numbers 13 and 14 occupied, the taller central facades. Number 14 was Miss Wakefield's ladies school, which was still listed a decade later. Richard Edwards continued his working interest in the Terrace, and in Folthorp's 1850 directory he is living at number 50, listed as a builder and surveyor. However, Mrs. Frances Kemp, and her late husband's two brothers-in-law (from Kemp's first marriage) the Barings, retained an interest and possibly provided some finance for the development. No doubt they also had control of the overall design of the facades. The deeds also show the further involvement of Edward and Henry Faithfull, Yearsley's partners in Powis Villas. While one of the builders, Edwards, lived in 1 Clifton Terrace, by 1856 his partner, G.W. Sawyer was living in Victoria House, Victoria Place, from where he conducted his carpentry and building business, also acting as a builder's merchant.

These members of the Faithfull and Baring families formed the group of evangelicals which, with the Kemps, seceded from the Church of England in 1816 and formed their own short-lived sect. The Barings were still involved with Kemp's second wife, maybe through a sense of loyalty and their religious ties, plus the fact that on his death Kemp owed a good deal of money to his first wife's estate. To help finance Kemp Town, Thomas Read had borrowed £42,000 from the trustees of his first marriage settlement. He had also obtained a further £24,000 from Henry Baring in 1832, (Dale 1967). As a result of Kemp's loans three members of the Baring family owned houses in Kemp Town during the first half of the nineteenth century (note 1).

For a last nostalgic look over Church Hill, before the developers move in, the 1839 *Stranger's Guide in Brighton* paints an interesting picture. On page 67 the Guide takes us on a 'Ramble to the Devil's Dyke':

'Passing over Church-hill, and leaving that edifice on the right . . the farm called New England is seen, in the hollow . . Nearly opposite New England, the road branches off to right and left; the former to Cuckfield and Lewes . . the latter for Portslade, Shoreham, Steyning etc. A road to Preston also branches off to the right'.

At New England was the dairy farm for the Prince of Wales, and it is interesting to notice the telling absence of any mention of the Church Hill Workhouse in the text of the guide.

In this 1839 guide's description of the various routes can be seen the origins of New England Road, Prestonville Road, and the junction of roads that established the Seven Dials that we know today. Having come over the top of Church Hill, the site of this divergence of roads is quite logical, as many of the traveller's destinations became visible from the high flat plain on which the Seven Dials roundabout now stands. From here could be seen Hove, Portslade, Blatchington, the River Adur, Shoreham, Preston, and the final hill on the way to Lewes. New England Road, leading into Chatham Place today, originally led from Preston to the chalybeate spring and was first called Wick Road.

J.G. Bishop (1880) adds some more names to this area, although his dates are difficult – he writes about Montpelier Crescent being pleasant fields in 1850, which is not quite right. In passing he mentions the area known as Preston Circus and the bottom of New England Hill, and then mentions the 'pretty triangular field' at New England, in front of which was originally Murrell's farm, and subsequently Harry Pegg's farm. Bishop describes this farm as intact in 1850 and covered with houses in 1870. He then makes a direct reference to Powis/Clifton. While writing about the Seven Dials, he notes, 'All the handsome property now in that neighbourhood, as indeed much of that in Buckingham-place, etc., and from Clifton-place to West Hill-road (where Mr. Hodson's famous Black Mill formerly stood), is of modern growth, irrespective of the fine property erected . . . '

Regarding New England, in the 1840 Rate Book (ESRO BH/B/4/34/1) is listed 'New England Farm, House and land, arable land, pasture land – occupier William Hallett'. Twenty years later, in the New Street Plans (ESRO DB/D6/14) the 'New England Estate' is listed, and D. Friend submitted the plans to develop York Grove and New England Road on 18th July 1861. Mr. Goultry submitted plans for York Villas on 11th July 1862. Roads were usually built a year or two after plans had been submitted.

While at the Seven Dials it is worth quoting Ryman & Mead (1994): 'Lovers Walk footpath also ended here along the route of modern Stanford and Prestonville Road'. Today Lovers Walk takes us off the London Road opposite Preston Park, up steep steps and across the railway track to Stanford Road. But before the railway was built the 'lovers' walked from where the Seven Dials is now, down the side of the undeveloped hill and into the meadow lands that became Preston Park. It is interesting to read, in Bishop's *A Peep into the Past*, of the high esteem in which the housing development on Church Hill was held at the end of the century.

Having mentioned the Workhouse already, it is important to look at its effect on our area, and its almost un-noticed inclusion in various engravings. While it is not on the West Side, it was the major building on Church Hill for many years. Once built, it was described in Baxter's 1822 *Stranger's Guide* as having views 'as far as Beachy-head to the east, and the Isle of Wight to the west'. In fact it would have been Seaford Head that was visible to the east. And, as mentioned, most of the upper windows would have looked straight down on the Kemp's new home, the Temple.

In Saunders' 1837 Directory it was also noted that, 'At a short distance from the house an Infirmary has been built for the reception of the sick paupers'. The Infirmary is also mentioned in Wallis's 1836 guide. The entries make it

The drawing of Church Hill Workhouse as illustrated in Erredge's 'History of Brighton'.

sound as if the building was a later addition, but it would have been nearly contemporary with the building of the Workhouse.

Of the forty or so nineteenth century engravings of St. Nicholas' church, the Workhouse building, further up the hill and due north of the church, appears in the background of ten. The Robert Havell aquatint from Brayley's 'Topographical Sketches of Brighthelmstone' 1825, illustrated on the facing page, shows the most extensive representation of the Workhouse in any of the church engravings. Any such view of the Workhouse included in a print of St. Nicholas' would be the side and rear views, as the front of the building, illustrated above, was on what is now Dyke Road.

In the background of three of the many engravings of St. Nicholas' Church there is also a building bearing the name of 'Bennett – stonemason' over its front porch. In the *Stranger's Guide* of 1855 there is a small lithograph of St. Nicholas' (illustrated later in the chapter) which also shows the building of Bennett Stonemason behind the church. The Workhouse was built before Bennett moved into the premises opposite the church, and of the Workhouse the text in this guide reads, 'the house is 191 feet in length, and is divided into four distinct parts, in order to class its inmates in the most regular manner'.

It is an interesting experiment to stand in the southern graveyard of the church and look up at the building from the same angle as portrayed in some of these old engravings. According to the mid-nineteenth century artists, if you

'St. Nicholas' Church, Brighton' drawn and aquatinted by Robert Havell. Published in Brayley's 'Topographical Sketches of Brighthelmstone', 1825.

The workhouse is the large building on the right, behind the church.
The northern extension of the churchyard, on the north side of Church Street, had been opened in 1824, and is represented by what appears to be the flat expanse of land between the church and the Workhouse. The flat landscape on the left of the picture is the land later developed into Clifton Terrace. When local builders Sawyer and Edwards bought plots of this land, twenty-one years after this print was published, it was probably quite cheap because of the Workhouse just across the road. The tenement buildings, discussed later in this chapter, are just out of sight behind the church.

stood slightly south-east and looked past the tower to the left of the church you saw Bennett's stonemason building, and if you were south-west and looked past the nave to the right of the church you saw the Workhouse. From both positions Shelley's tenements are hidden behind the church itself. Keeping in mind the 1825 Robert Havell print mentioned above, standing by the church in the same position as the artist, his depiction of the Workhouse places it well beyond the house named 'Shelleys' in Mount Zion Place, and to the west of the present St. Nicholas Road, just south of the junction of where Buckingham Road now joins Dyke Road. The dwelling known as 'Shelleys' predates the Workhouse by two decades. It was built about 1801 as the home of William Shelley, the Beadle to St. Nicholas', who arranged many of the day-to-day events in the parish. Shelley took over the position of Beadle from Thomas Waring in 1801, so it appears the house was built for Shelley himself. In Baxter's New Brighton Directory of 1822 the listing reads 'Sion Place – number of houses 13, William Shelley – sexton'. By 1846 the occupant is the Rev. Henry Stewart Byron, and it is referred to as Sion House (Kelly's 1846 Directory). However, Shelley had other interests in the area, and in 1840 he is recorded as something of an established landlord. In the 1840 Burial Ground Rate Book (ESRO BH/B/4/34/1) Mount Zion Place is listed as tenements, with William Shelley as the landlord. In the 1854 Town Rate Book (ESRO BH/B/4/37/2) it is listed as Mount Sion Place, with numbers 2,3,4 & 5 of the tenements still owned by Shelley.

Returning to the stonemason's business, the Brighton street directories confirm Bennett's presence on Church Hill and they list the following references to his premises:

Folthorp's Directory 1850
Benjamin Bennett
2 Centurion Place, Stonemason and Statuary.
1 Centurion Place was Wm. Buckman (no trade mentioned)

Taylor's Directory 1854
Benj. Bennett 41 Church Street.
Also describes Centurion Place as 'a part of Church Street opposite St. Nicholas' Church', confirmed on the 1853 map illustrated in chapter 6.

Folthorp's 1856
Church Street 41 B. Bennett
Centurion Place is listed as 'on Church Hill, opposite the north side of the Parish Church, now numbered in Church Street'.
Centurion Road is noted as 'facing the north front of the parish church'.

Folthorp's 1864
Centurion Place noted as 'small private houses'
Church Street — 41 B. Bennett stonemason.

Undoubtedly many of the gravestones to St. Nicholas' would have been supplied by Bennett's, and perhaps the large stone eagle above the door of 9 Clifton Road, mentioned in chapter 4, was their work as well. In the illustration on page 35 showing Bennett's premises behind the tower of the church, the Workhouse does not appear in the full print as it would have been completely obscured by the church itself from the artist's angle. This places the business premises of the stonemason on the northern corner of Church Street and Dyke

Road, on that piece of the northern burial ground by the gated southern entrance where today the land is substantially higher than the pavement. Interestingly, there are few graves on that piece of ground today, and nineteenth century maps of the area occasionally have an un-named building on that corner. The Index of New Street Plans (ESRO DB/D6/14) indicates that Bennett himself was behind the development of St. Nicholas Road. In the plans St. Nicholas Road is presented to the council as a proposed new street by 'Bennett and others' on 24th June 1866. In the church print just mentioned it appears as if Bennett's premises would have had to be knocked down to make way for St. Nicholas Road, so some time between the Folthorp business entry of 1864, and by the time the 1866 plans were accepted, Bennett presumably ended his stonemasonry business on Church Hill and Shelley's tenements were demolished.

These details of Bennett's business premises and Shelley's tenement buildings finally shed light on the strange building seen in the background of the following two engravings, the first by Whittock, 1829, and the second by Sickelmore of 'Brighton Church' published in 1824. With that early date these buildings pre-date Bennett's involvement, Shelley had been the Beadle for over twenty years, and the Workhouse, further up the hill, was about three years old. Because the church commissioners were responsible for the Workhouse, the most likely origin of these tenements was that they were built at much the same time as the Workhouse itself, early 1820s, as a staging-post for getting inmates out of that institution and back into the working community, together with others who maybe had work but were temporarily without a home. The process would have been overseen by the landlord, William Shelley, and the 1825 Pigott-Smith map suggests these tenements were quite large, extending northwards round the corner and into Mount Zion Place. This poses other questions, because Shelley himself lived in Mount Zion Place, and later on the artist R.H. Nibbs also lived there. A possible explanation is that, in its early days, the name 'Mount Zion Place' encompassed an area to the north of the church that may have included two roads.

Detail of J. Rogers' steel engraving of St. Nicholas' Church, after N. Whittock – published in 1829.
Behind the church can be seen the same building that appears in the next view after Sickelmore.

"Brighton Church" Aquatint engraving published in Sickelmore's
'Descriptive Views of Brighton' 1824.

In this engraving of St. Nicholas' Church, the artist was standing where the western burial ground is today.
The view shows the junction of the top of Church Street and Dyke Road, then called the Road from
Steyning, with Shelley's tenements far left.

From the 1839 Directory it also appears that Bennett had a shop at 34 North Lane, where his business is described as 'Stone and Marble Masons', but the family had been in business long before that. In T.H. Boore's Brighton Annual Directory of 1822 Benjamin Bennett is at 48 Middle Street, listed as a builder and carpenter, and in the 1832 Brighton Directory he is listed as a lime burner of 44/45 Middle Street. Presumably this was the father, because in the same directory Benjamin Bennett junior is at 65 Church Street as a stone mason. It is difficult to establish how much the numbering of Church Street changed during these years, but maybe by 1850 his father had died and Bennett junior was looking for larger premises and an increase in the number of workers needed for the hard graft of shaping up the rough stones. The solution was to take over the western end of Mr. Shelley's tenements, and his enlarged work force would be next door.

The track-way that preceded Church Street, running up from the Steine to join the Road to Steyning, does not appear on the c1740 map of Brighton Parish, but is in place, although unnamed, on Budgen's 1788 map. It is still unnamed on Yeakell and Gardner's map of 1779, and in fact the track shown on many of these maps was usually Spring Walk. When the Church Street route was established it started just a little to the south of Spring Walk (Ford 1981), and it was finally named as Church Street by the Town Commissioners in 1792. The early name of Spring Walk for this route indicated it was a pathway to get from the Steine to the Chalybeate at St. Ann's Well.

At the southern end of the churchyard Wykeham Terrace was built from 1827 over a period of about a decade, and by the 1840s Dyke Road, going up the western side of the burial ground, was described as 'Church Hill and Road, leading from the Parish Church and Cemetery direct to the Dyke Road' (Folthorp's 1848 Directory). The name of Dyke Road actually started much nearer the brow of Church Hill, with Vine Cottage and the Workhouse listed as being on Church Hill, not Dyke Road, which name seems to have started about where the Buckingham Road turning is today. Norman Villa (now St. George's House), the large house on the southern corner of Clifton Terrace, was built c1847, the year after a start was made on the Terrace itself. At much the same time a house named Grosmont Villa, occupied by J. Collingwood Esq. was also listed on Church Hill, but to date its location is not confirmed. It is most likely to be the house immediately beside Vine's Cottage, now the offices of the Clifton Design Associates. From the Directory's description it seems Grosmont was north of Vine's Cottage because by Folthorp's 1850 Directory it is listed in Dyke Road, which indicates that by this time the name 'Dyke Road' had started creeping down towards the town, and replacing the name Church Hill. If Grosmont Villa had been any further north than this it would never have had Church Hill as its original address. In the 1861 census the listing is 'Grosmont Villa with Stables' and today there appear to be buildings behind the Clifton Design house that could have been the stables.

The next building on this side was the Church Hill School House, and there were no private buildings on the other side of the road: it was all grounds of the Workhouse. Also by 1856, for a short time at the lowest end of Church Hill, there was a small inn called the Buckingham Arms, with G. Wood as the landlord, listed in Folthorp's Directory of that date. It probably served the coach passengers who had to disembark to enable the horses to get the coach up the hill, and who needed a drink before walking up the hill themselves.

In the following view from the tower of St. Nicholas' Church, that part of the present Dyke Road that was called Church Hill is in the foreground. Clifton Terrace, on the far right, is about four years old, with Norman Villa and its Italianate tower in front of it. Saxon Villa on the far corner of the Terrace grounds had not been built yet. Saxon Villa was a flint stone house on the site of the modern block of flats in Clifton Place. It was originally owned by Marriage Wallis, the treasurer of the Soup Fund, for the poor of Brighton, and of a charity called the Jubilee and Accidental Fund, of 14 Market Street. Wallis was a local philanthropist who was one of the original trustees of the Brighton and Sussex Equitable Permanent Benefit Building Society, established in the town

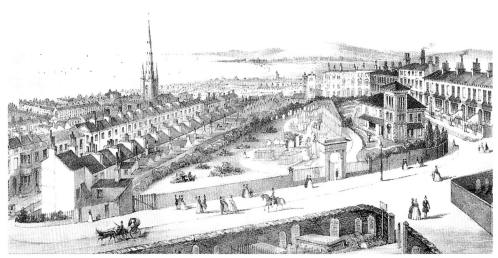

'West View of Brighton from the
top of the Old Church'.
Lithograph by J. Newman,
published by W. Grant c 1850.

in 1863. The business is now the Alliance & Leicester. The western burial ground in the centre of the scene was opened ten years earlier. Upper North Street is well portrayed, but St. Mary Magdalen Church was not yet built, so the rather exaggerated spire is that of Christ Church in Montpelier Road. Despite the fact that Powis is not seen, nor Clifton Hill itself, this print represents the most comprehensive view of our area, Church Hill – West Side.

Note the attractive bow-fronted terraced homes where the present office block at the eastern end of Upper North Street now stands. The Buckingham Arms was possibly the building shown on the northern corner of Upper North Street and Church Hill, with the stark white side wall and the small courtyard buildings behind it.

Detail of St. Nicholas' from 'The Stranger's Guide to Brighton' 1855 showing the title 'Bennett Stonemason' above the door of the large building behind the church.

The only known nineteenth century image of Shelley's cottage appears in another of the engravings of St. Nicholas'. The cottage is in Richard Henry Nibbs' line engraving of the church from his series 'Churches of Sussex', published in 1851. The print, illustrated below, is entitled 'Brighton' and shows Shelley's at the far right of the scene.

Shelley's Cottage

Richard Henry Nibbs' line engraving of St. Nicholas', from his series 'Churches of Sussex', published in 1851. Nibbs would probably have known Shelley: they were near neighbours during the early 1840s when Nibbs lived at 11 Mount Zion Place.

Erredge (1862) states that the Workhouse architect was William Mackie of Charlotte Street, Blackfriars Road, London, his design being selected by the directors from forty other submissions. John Cheesman was the builder – and the directors ensured it combined the 'correct degree of elegance with economy'. Erredge noted that it had 95 inmates, although other later figures were much higher.

The Workhouse dominated the church and the top of Church Hill, overlooking the town for several decades from the early 1820s, but the fact that there is no specific engraving of the building illustrates the, quite understandable, selective nature of the artistic representation of the town and its buildings. This commercially driven selective nature extends to the artistic exclusion of much of the Clifton/ Montpelier/Powis development itself, which, compared with other, older areas of the town, gained very little attention from the mid-nineteenth century artists. A glance at the range of Brighton prints illustrates this. By 1853 the last houses in Powis Villas were completed, being the terrace of four at the southern end, and between 1852 and 1854 the residents in Powis Square went up from seven to seventeen, according to the street directories. Looking at the domestic houses in Brighton represented by lithograph or steel engraving around this time, there is, among others, Charles Freshfield's Pennant Lodge, and Thomas Attree's house, 1863, (both near Queens Park), Lewes Crescent and Marine Square, both published by Rock & Co 1853-1860, 6 Pavilion Buildings 1865, Meeting House Lane 1860, Nos. 137 & 138 Marine Parade in 1845, and Lion Mansion 1865. Yet no engravings of houses or scenes in Powis Square, Powis Villas, Clifton Hill or Clifton Road, Montpelier Villas or Montpelier Terrace were ever published. While these addresses are held in high esteem today, they were not originally built as houses for the gentry, nor were they particularly grand, so to the artists, publishers and their clients of the day they were apparently of little interest.

Rather this area was built by and for trades-people, businessmen, craftsmen and the builders themselves, and it represented a significant change in the social group that now saw itself as property developers. And of course, with this particular social mix, the proximity of the Workhouse was not so socially inappropriate as it would have been were it built just across the road from, say, Sussex Square. But in fact, by 1870 when the Workhouse had been demolished and the villas of Buckingham and Leopold Roads were developed on its grounds, the area had become much more desirable than it was in 1850 when Clifton/Powis was being built. Unfortunately from the print historian's point of view the era of the English topographical engraving was coming to an end by the late 1860s. So apart from the type of houses and the social class of the new residents of Church Hill putting off the print publishers of the day, by the time that that ceased to be a problem, and the area was seen as more desirable, the topographical print market was fast disappearing, to be replaced by the late Victorian and early Edwardian black and white photograph. Thus the Church Hill development fell between two stools and was never recorded. Yearsley with his partners, the Baring family, Henry Faithfull and local enterprising builders like the Halletts, were the pioneers who led the middle classes out of the old town and up Church Hill, but the artists and engravers never followed.

However, the two social classes of Clifton Hill and Sussex Square were soon given the opportunity to enjoy Brighton together, as John Farrant (2005) notes in his reprint of Erredge. In 1848 the Royal Estates decided to sell the Royal Pavilion, and the town voted to borrow the money to buy it. In 1862 Erredge recorded that the debt was being reduced, and the town had an extensive park of its own in its very centre. He applauded the fact that 'since 1851 numerous balls, concerts and meetings of various societies have taken place there, and it now has an excellent gallery for paintings, and several rooms have been set aside for the Brighton Museum. . . the tradesman/businessman and his wife' (precisely those people who had built, and now lived on Church Hill) 'and their children could now pass an edifying Sunday afternoon where once royalty frolicked'. Dinkel (1983) describes the town's purchase of the Royal Pavilion as 'a remarkable early instance of municipal conservation'. The new Brightonians of Church Hill went to this exciting cultural centre to see flower shows, visit artists' studios, attend lectures and go to charity balls and concerts.

With the Workhouse remaining in use on Church Hill until the end of 1867, although the final decision to sell had been taken in 1853, it meant that just across Dyke Road the new developments of Clifton Terrace and Powis Grove were being built while the business of the Workhouse was in full swing. The easternmost houses of Clifton Terrace, nos. 1 & 2 (closest to the Workhouse) were built in 1846, and the new residents of the Terrace and the Grove lived just across the road from this institution for another twenty years. Mr. Vine the miller also experienced the Workhouse being built literally the other side of the road from his home. John Yearsley was on the committee appointed in May 1852 to report on the disposal of the workhouse and the building of its replacement on Elm Grove (Martin 1871), although he died long before any progress was made.

In the early 1800s the number of poor citizens claiming relief was rising at an alarming rate, and this necessitated the passing of the Poor Law Amendment Act of 1834. One of its objectives was to encourage administrators to make their workhouses the most unpleasant places possible, to deter people from seeking shelter. Another objective was to empower and encourage the Poor Law Commissioners to provide education for workhouse children. Married couples were generally separated. Any children were taken from them and usually educated outside the Workhouse premises, hence the Church Hill School House run by the Rev. Dr. William Henry Butler – although the Workhouse did have its own school room, probably for the youngest children.

People wanting to visit anyone in the Church Hill Workhouse had to obtain an order from the Director, a Guardian or an Overseer, and the only visiting time allowed was between 2pm and 4pm on Thursdays. Later in the book, in connection with the amount of building going on in the area by the 1850s, the point is made that able-bodied men from the Workhouse would almost certainly have been sent out to work on the local building sites, to help pay for their keep. The inmates' work inside the Workhouse included grinding their own corn for baking, making their own clothing, producing whiting for laundries, dressing flax and carding wool, and making rope, cord, door mats, rugs and sacking of every description, (Wallis 1836). In *Taylor's Royal Brighton Guide* 1844 he writes that the 'Workhouse soil is very favourable to the production of vegetables, considerable quantities of which are sold in the market. The house has often been visited by the nobility and gentry, who have expressed their admiration at the perfect order and cleanliness in which it is kept . . . (and that the) Governor's and Matron's exertions add greatly to the comfort and health of the inmates'. Dale (1976) tells us that the Workhouse housed 600 inmates, and in 1848 the directors and guardians were recommended by a special committee to extend the building at the estimated cost of £1,749. 12s, in order to accommodate 300 more people, but in the end no action was taken.

Once the new Workhouse at the top of Elm Grove was in use, by the September of 1867, the old site on Church Hill and its extensive grounds was sold and redeveloped with the roads named after the Royal Family – Albert Road, Alexandra, Alfred and Leopold. Just a little further up Church Hill from the Workhouse, Erredge writes about a cattle market that was established on a piece of the parish ground on the Church Hill, adjoining the West Hill estate, in 1831. It must have been outside the northern boundary of the Workhouse grounds, near Hodson's Mill, but lasted only a few years, there being no meadows near for the keeping of stock. He also writes that the 'Manor Pound' (for impounding cattle) was at the back of the parish church, on the spot now occupied by the northern burial ground, which site also included the parish stocks for some years. In 1824, when the church extended its graveyard to the north of Church Street, this pound was moved up to the north-west corner of the Workhouse grounds, on the Dyke Road just south of the cattle market. It can be seen in the 1846 Nibbs print illustrated at the end of this chapter. It lasted longer than the cattle market, but by 1853 it had become obsolete and was purchased by the parish from the Lord of the Manor for £100. Erredge would have known this area particularly well as he moved from 1 Wykeham Terrace to live in West Hill Street in March 1858.

Prior to the new Elm Grove Workhouse becoming functional in 1867, the children had already been moved from Church Hill, up over Race Hill to the newly built Warren Farm Industrial School. D'Enno (2004) records that on August 14th 1862 '77 boys and 65 girls marched in procession, under the supervision of Mr. & Mrs. Hales the first superintendents, from the Church Hill Workhouse to Warren Farm'. By this time it was thought inappropriate to continue keeping children in a workhouse with adults. The whole move took about ten days. To gain an impression of the Church Hill Workhouse, it was similar in front elevation to its replacement on Elm Grove, the present Brighton General Hospital. The hospital is just a little taller, perhaps two more floors, and both institutions offered their inmates beautiful views over the town. In its final months on Church Hill, the Commissioners in Lunacy reported to the Lord Chancellor that the Workhouse was home to 20 'insane, idiotic and imbecile inmates'.

When its closure finally came, a report of the auction of the Workhouse buildings and grounds was reported in *The Builder* magazine of March 1868, and it shows the remarkable change in attitudes to the area. In chapter 9 reference is made to Erredge's description of the 'howling wilderness of Church Hill' when the Workhouse was built in 1821. Forty-seven years later *The Builder* mentions that the land was restricted to the building of villas, and reports, 'This was the only opportunity of obtaining land for villas in the centre of the town and away from the bustle of business. The situation is about the highest point of Brighton, commanding a view of the sea, the Downs and the town; it is in close proximity to the railway and parish church, and abuts onto one of the principal pleasure rides and drives in the borough, namely the Dyke-road'. Such was the change in sentiment towards living on Church Hill, which was now considered part of the 'centre of town'.

One of the largest plots, from the 38 on offer in the auction, was on the southern corner of Buckingham Road and Dyke Road. George Attree, an auctioneer of North Street, was the successful bidder, at £800. The total realised for the Workhouse buildings, which would have included the separate Infirmary, all of which needed demolishing, together with the many acres of land, was £31,524. Only twenty-one years earlier John Yearsley had bought nearly three acres just the other side of Dyke Road for £2,100. In the Index of New Streets (ESRO DB/D6/14) the location is listed as 'The Workhouse Estate' and on 26th September 1868 Mr. Maynard submitted three lithographs detailing the proposed new streets of Albert Road, Alexandra Villas, Alfred Road, Leopold Road, Buckingham Road and Buckingham Street. To get three prints published, detailing the development of six streets, with one of them well over a quarter of a mile long, just six months after the auction, implies Mr. Maynard had started work on the plans before the auction sale came up.

The following detail is the right hand side of the print illustrated on page 42, and the artist is standing on the later site of West Hill Road. The tower of St. Nicholas' Church, with the flag flying, is on the skyline in the far right distance. In front and to the right of the church are the three gable roofs of the back of the Workhouse, and in front of that, on the right hand edge of the picture, is the tall red-roofed building of the Infirmary, with the three side windows in a vertical line and the sun shining on the upper part of the side wall. This is the only known image of the infirmary in a Brighton print. All workhouses throughout the country were obliged to have an infirmary, and in the eighteenth century institutions they were part of the main building. By the early nineteenth century, for the purposes of better infection control, they were usually separate buildings.

Detail from the lithograph by C. Childs after a sketch by R.H. Nibbs entitled
'View of Brighton from Hudson's Mill'. Published Jan. 1st 1846 by W.Lane,
3 Market Street.

The bottom right of this scene, a fenced area with animal stalls, would appear to be the Manor Cattle Pound that is quoted from Erredge. The land being farmed in the foreground and middle distance is all part of the nine acres that belonged to the Workhouse. Again, this very rare lithograph is the only known image of the inmates working the land. Nibbs (1816–1893) described by Ford (1981) as the most distinguished local artist, lived at 7 Buckingham Place for the last twenty years of his life, but his chosen subject matter was usually the mundane and ordinary, rather than the fine and elegant buildings and fashionable figures of so many Brighton publications. It is quite likely that very few copies of this scene were ever printed and sold, because of its subject matter. The full print below shows the land on which Buckingham Road, St. Nicholas Road, Albert and Alfred Roads were later built. Also depicted is a line of roofs descending away from the church in the right-hand middle distance, which is Kew Street running into North Gardens. Exactly twenty years later that view would be obscured by St. Nicholas Road.

Above is the complete view of the 1846 lithograph after R.H. Nibbs entitled 'View of Brighton from Hudson's Mill'. On the far left is Brighton Station beyond which St. Peter's Church can just be seen. In the left hand foreground, the diagonal footpath with the flint-stone wall runs across where Albert Road is today, and it seems to join up near the top of Guildford Road, the houses of which can be seen leading down the hill to the station.

3

The Churches of the Area

The period from 1840 to the mid 1870s saw the building of thirteen Anglican churches in Brighton, doubling the number in the town. Five churches were added to our area, one Catholic in Upper North Street, a Congregational Church, one Non-Conformist and two Anglican.

The original parish church of St. Nicholas pre-dates this busy period of church building. Antony Dale in *The History & Architecture of Brighton* tells us that 'The Domesday survey records a church at Brighton in the 11th century, without saying where it was'. The present church dates from the extensive rebuilding in 1853 of the original construction of c1350. However, F. Harrison and J.S.North (1937) make the suggestion that this early Domesday church was on the site of the present St. Nicholas'. Writing about Church Hill, they say:

' . . . from the many finds of burials, ornaments and masses of stones . . . it is evident that Church-hill was venerated as a sacred mount, and here was the early open-air church, which later became the site of the first building mentioned in the Domesday Survey. The present building was started in the mid 14th century'.

If this part of Church Hill was viewed as a sacred mount, it is easy to agree with Harrison and North's suggestion that the 14th century building was indeed erected on the site of the 11th century church. A peal of eight bells, cast by a foundry in Bristol, was hung in St. Nicholas' in 1777. Two additional bells were added in 1818 but later transferred to St. Peter's, (Fleet 1847). Baxter's *Stranger in Brighton Guide* of 1822 tells us that 'The peal is very musical, and the town is often enlivened with its harmony'.

T.W. Hemsley, a verger of the church, wrote *A Short History of, and Guide Book to, St. Nicholas' Church, Brighton* in 1896, and his work re-inforces Harrison and North's ideas. He suggests there is 'every reason to suppose' the early 11th century church stood on the present site and that 'evidence points to a larger, instead of a smaller structure than the present, and to a more elaborate building, and in the Norman style of architecture'. He re-tells the story that during the 1853 restoration, in taking down the corner stones on the buttresses to the tower, 'many of the stones were discovered to be carved with Norman ornaments which had been turned inward, and the carved parts – originally the exterior – buried in the mortar'. He also uses the evidence of the well-known picture map of the French attack on Brighthelmstone in 1545. The church is represented 'as surrounded by soldiers with spears . . and persons . . in the attitude of prayer. The church is of a large size, with circular tower' which is 'pierced with a row of Norman windows, or portholes, and all the windows in the building are Norman'. Hemsley then questions Erredge's (1862) thoughts that the picture is not a reliable representation of the church, and writes that 'it is at least exceedingly likely to have been correct in its main features' – in other words, it was a Norman church.

The following illustration is a sepia etching by W.T. Quatermain, showing how St. Nicholas' was reduced to just a shell before being re-built, following the plans of Richard Cromwell Carpenter, in 1853-54. Quartermain was an amateur artist who was the inspector for the Corporation Fire Brigade at 115 Western Road in the 1860s, and the inspector in the Office for Testing Gas Meters, in Bartholomews. This view is taken from the north and we can see straight through the central aisle of the church to the sea beyond, such was the extent of the re-building. The block of dark stone on the right hand edge is the

'Brighton, St. Nicholas' Church, During the Restoration, 1853.'
'The work started on June 3rd 1853 and ended on March 10th 1854.
About fifty men were employed daily in the work, no accident
happily occurring during its progress.' Hemsley (1896).
The total cost was £5,769. 18s 7d. The architect, Carpenter,
died soon after the restored church was opened.

old tower. Prior to this restoration, Hemsley quotes 'a graphic sketch, by an old inhabitant, of the old parish church' – 'Dear homely Church; crazy, unsafe, unsanitary, it may have been; embedded in graves, with tombstones almost blocking up the windows. No doubt it is vastly improved in every respect; but there was a snug family feeling about the old Church of my boyhood's days that it is pleasant to remember after all.'

The five other churches which were part of this nineteenth century burst of ecclesiastical building work were Clifton Road Congregational Church, All Saints' in Compton Avenue, St.Michael and All Angels' in Victoria Road, Christ Church in Montpelier Road and St. Mary Magdalen's in Upper North Street.

Clifton Road Congregational Church, on the corner of Clifton Road and Dyke Road, was built by Thomas Simpson and registered for worship in 1870. In the decade before the church was pulled down the Children's Hospital always held their Christmas Party in its basement. In the *Argus* of 4th February 2006 Adam Trimingham wrote 'A landmark in Brighton was the Dials Congregational Church on top of the hill in Dyke Road. It could be seen for miles with its 150ft tall tower, described by Ken Fines (2004) as "one of the finest landmarks on Brighton's skyline",

Above left: Clifton Road Congregational Church, where Clifton Road meets Dyke Road, the site of Homelees House today.

Left: The interior of Clifton Road Congregational Church.

45

but it was knocked down in 1972, and replaced by Homelees House.' Musgrave (1981) describes it as one of the most important of Brighton's late Victorian nonconformist churches, with its remarkable circular interior.

The second church was All Saints', Compton Avenue (previously part of Clifton Road) registered for public worship in 1853, having been built in 1852 and demolished in 1957. Writing in 1862 Erredge notes 'the spire remains as yet unfinished'. Erredge goes on to describe the church as 'a fine specimen of the Early English style, built of flintstone and with a fine toned organ. It was built in 1852 by Mr. Cheesman, the architect being R.C. Carpenter – the Rev. Thos. Coombe MA of Trinity College, Cambridge, is the priest'. The Church Hall still stands behind the original site of the church, and its foundation stone reads 'All Saints Church – Sunday School Room, Foundation stone laid 4th July 1900 by T.P.Baptie DL. JP. Incumbent Rev. F.H.T. Curtis'.

Interior of All Saints', Compton Avenue.

The third church, the first and smaller version of St. Michael and All Angels', had its foundation stone laid on 29th September 1861, from designs drawn by G.F. Bodley in 1858. The interior work was given to the company newly formed by William Morris, and was that company's first large scale commission. It was built for the Rev. Charles Beanlands, who was himself interested in church design, and was the first red-brick church in Brighton. Sir Roy Strong describes it as 'A Pre-Raphaelite jewel, one of England's grandest Victorian churches'. In his *History and Guide to St. Michael's*, David Beevers (1993) writes that it was while the Rev. Beanlands was the curate at St. Paul's Church in Brighton that he first met the architect G.F.Bodley. The Rev. Henry Wagner created the new parish of Montpelier, and the total cost of building the new church was £6,728. Two rich spinster sisters, Mary and Sarah Windle donated most of the money, both for the original building and for the enlarged church. Wagner & Dale (1983) write about the very 'high church spirit' of the ritual in the services at St. Michael's. In 1865 the Rev. Wagner was reluctantly prompted to question

Beanlands, and other parishes, regarding the increasing introduction of ritual. It must have been even higher than Wagner's style of churchmanship, and he asked for a requisition in favour of the services that had to be signed by twelve property-owning members of the congregation. Beanlands' curate, the Rev. Thomas Walter Perry, came up with an endorsement of the rituals signed by one hundred householders, so the matter was dropped.

The larger extension to the north of the church was designed by William Burges in 1868, but building did not commence until twenty-five years later, with the foundation stone being laid by Lady Troubridge on 26th July 1893.

Many of the windows in the extension were by Charles Eamer Kempe & Company, whose founder was the eldest son of Nathaniel Kemp. Musgrave (1981) makes the point that it was realized the original church was too small as soon as it opened, but this was not necessarily a lack of foresight by Beanlands. He would surely have known that the surrounding fields would be built on, but might have made the reasonable assumption that the new homes would follow the pattern of the small detached or semi-detached villas that were in the area

'St. Michael and All Angels' Church, Brighton'
Steel engraving published by Rock & Co. London, 13 July 1866.
(Illustrated larger than the original size)

already. The tall high-density terraces that quite quickly landed on his doorstep must have been a shock to the parish church (St. Michael's Place is discussed in chapter 6). The engraving (previous page) of the first smaller church building, is dated 1866. On the far left of this picture is the back of 8 Powis Road, and the following detail of the print illustrates what is now the barber's shop on the corner of Powis Road.

1866

2006

Detail of the above engraving of St. Michael and All Angels',
Victoria Road, compared with the view as it is today.

This rare engraving, on page 47, shows the church before its enlargement. On the left-hand side can be seen the back of the southern most house in Powis Road. This is the only known engraved image of this church, all other publications being photographic. The publisher, Rock & Co. started producing illustrated letter paper in 1839 and their venture was greatly helped by the introduction of the Penny Post the following year. Eventually Rock produced over seven thousand different illustrations for letter headings, and from 1849 had to start numbering them to facilitate repeat orders. This print is number 5628. Rock produced many images of churches, and as St. Michael's must have caused quite a stir when it was built, it is difficult to know whether Rock produced this image independently, or if the Rev. Beanlands commissioned it. What is surely certain is that it must have been used by Beanlands as his letter heading for many years.

The left-hand illustration (above) shows the corner of Powis Road and

Victoria Road in 1866, and part of the terrace on the northern side of Victoria Road. It also tells us that the present corner premises of Headroom the barbers was a shop in 1866. The present address of Headroom is 22 Victoria Road, but in the street directories of the 1860s the numbers of Victoria Road only go up to 18. In Kelly's 1862 Directory No. 4 Victoria Road is entered as 'Thomas Robson – chemist, druggist, and Post Office Receiving House' – and the assumption is that this is now the premises of Headroom the barbers.

Before the post office run by the late Mr. Doshi was opened in Clifton Hill, the local Post Office was at the 2007 address of Headroom (which is why the post box is there). So it may be reasonable to assume that the present 22 is the past number 4, and that in the 1860s when the church was built, the present barber shop was Mr. Robson's chemist, who also took in and distributed the local mail. In the 1855 *Stranger's Guide in Brighton* there are listed ten Receiving Houses for mail in Brighton, and the hours of posting in Victoria Road were 9.15am, 1.45, 5.45 and 8pm. By Kelly's 1867 Directory it has been re-numbered to 3 Victoria Road, and it also acted as a Money Order Office and a Post Office Savings Bank.

The Rev. Charles Beanlands was the first priest-in-charge of St. Michael and All Angels', and he moved into his new vicarage, Victoria House, Victoria Place, from Western Cottages, in late 1866. Victoria House pre-dates the church and the deeds confirm that it was not built as the vicarage, but started life as the home and workshop of a carpentry and building business, and it was not the first house to be built in Victoria Place. In the 1841 census this street had one cottage, occupied by a labourer and his laundress wife. Two more houses are noted as in the process of being built. By the 1854 Town Rate Book (ESRO BH/B/4/37/2) numbers 2 and 3 are occupied by Charles Stoner and Joseph Mandell respectively. Number 1, Victoria House, is owned by Henry Corney who eventually sells to Beanlands, while number 4 is a storehouse owned by Charles Jones. It was this premises that was the first Victoria Place house, occupied by the labourer and his wife in 1841. From the description in the census record, houses 2 and 3 were the next to be built, and Victoria House was the last, which did not appear in the 1841 census.

Many of the deeds to Victoria House are still in the private collection with the house, and the earliest deed, of May 1810, refers to the will of Thomas Kemp (T.R's father) regarding land called Wall Furlong, West Laine, Hilly Laine and Chalk Pit Furlong (where Corp Staines lived). It also refers to the earlier owners mentioned in chapter 1, the Duke of Dorset, Charles Callis Western, who had title on 8th May 1794, and Thomas Friend. Another land owner from a later deed, in or just before 1819, was William Bendall. An 1835 document refers to 16 parcels of land in the furlong next to West Fields in West Laine, with the builder Francis Hallett as a leaseholder to T.R. Kemp for 99 years, with restrictions that 'nothing unsightly' is built, and nothing below a value of £400. It also makes reference to the land south of a road that leads from the Temple to the Workhouse. This road has earlier been identified as Victoria Road and Vine Place, and so establishes our location as the land now occupied by Montpelier Street and Victoria Street.

It is assumed that Francis Hallett was William Hallett's father, and Francis seems to become more of a landlord and leaseholder while his son was busy building properties along Upper North Street. The above mentioned 1835 agreement, with Francis Hallett signing up to 'nothing unsightly' and to particular values of properties, does not seem to have been immediately acted upon on the land to the north of Upper North Street. The late 1830s is certainly before any development took place in the Victoria and Montpelier Street area, and as will be seen in chapter 10, William the son was busy building along Upper North Street before housing moved up towards the top of Church Hill – West Side.

Just prior to Yearsley's purchase to develop the Clifton/Powis area in 1846, these lower slopes of Chalk Pit Furlong and West Laine on Church Hill were becoming an area of intense activity. In the list of builders in the directories of this time are many of the names involved with the later development at the top of the hill, and all moving in to 'live on the job' of developing these lower southern slopes of Church Hill. While George Cheesman jnr was living at 156 Western Road, Richard Edwards was at 2 Upper North Street with Francis Hallett at 28, William Hallett was in 7 Hampton Place in 1832 and built 88 Upper North Street, and George W. Sawyer was living at 87 Upper North Street. Given that Sawyer was a carpenter living next door to number 88, which William Hallett built, it is likely that Sawyer was one of Hallett's many carpenters. William Wisden was at 31 Crown Street and Thomas Wisden was at 15 Hampton Place. Thomas Wisden, the builder of many of our local houses, had moved from 69 John Street, where he lived in 1833, and by 1844 was at 8 Victoria Street, then on to Hampton Place the year later. Also in 1832 Joseph Wisden, builder, is living at 18 Norfolk Square.

While Francis Hallett entered into the leasehold agreement with Kemp, it was William who did much of the development, and the lease agreement with Kemp obviously included permission for the Halletts to sell any pieces of land on which they built. This was an advantageous arrangement that Hallett father and son had agreed with Kemp, enabling them to keep any development of this area in the family, or extend opportunities to their friends or preferred business partners as they saw fit. No-one else could 'muscle in' and buy land over their heads, as it was all leased by Francis, while his son clearly had first refusal on the development of any plot.

Returning to Victoria House, a deed dated 24th June 1846 mentions 9 and 10 Victoria Street and George Chapman as owner of the land, with a restriction of a building line in Victoria Street of 8 feet from the road. This is the covenant that established the depth of the front gardens of Victoria Street. A mortgage of 16th March 1849 mentions Victoria Place and a 'carpenter's shop and dwelling place' lived in by Thomas Willmott, but then bought by Robert Newman Esq. This is the first mention of Victoria House itself in the deeds, and so places the construction of the house between 1841 and 1846. This deed refers to 'a new street called Montpelier Street', and a 'new road, width of 30 feet, called Victoria Place, leading between Montpelier Street and Victoria Street'.

The next deed of 28th Jan 1856 refers to premises owned by Frederick Price Judson, with a plan showing a dwelling place (now Victoria House) a side entrance (now garage) leading to a builder's yard (now back garden) and a carpenter's shop (now summer house). It refers to a business partnership between George David Sawyer and George William Sawyer – carpenters and builders. Presumably they rented the premises and dwelling from Judson. G.W. Sawyer, with a previous business partner Richard Edwards, was involved in the building of Clifton Terrace in 1846, but prior to this enterprise Sawyer was already an established builder in the town. In the mid 1830s he had worked on houses in Brunswick Square, building numbers 16, 17 and 19 for a speculator called Charles Elliott. The agreement was that Sawyer would build a house 'for £3,000 to be finished complete, prepared, painted with all drains, stores and pavements, the fixtures to be set at Mr. Sawyer's expense' (The Regency Town House website – accessed 2007).

Back to Victoria House again, it is about ten years later that it is first linked to the church of St. Michael and All Angels. Capt. Boucher, 5th Regiment of Lancers, of Moor House, Droxford, Hants, owned the house for two days from 31st October to 2nd November 1866 and then sold it to the Rev. Chas. Beanlands for £1,025 freehold. The Rev. Beanlands MA (of Clare College, Cambridge) was living at 5 Western Cottages, and listed in Kelly's Directory as the priest at St. Michael's. Western Cottages is now Sillwood Road: it was re-named in the early 1870s. Interestingly, it was in Western Cottages, as a guest of Kemp's sister, Mrs. Ann Sober, that John Constable and his wife Maria and family stayed during their visit to Brighton in 1824, during which time Constable painted the windmills on Church Hill. This ownership of Victoria House by Capt. Boucher for just two days is strange. Maybe he had to buy quickly, on behalf of Beanlands, in order to secure the premises for the church. A couple of years later Capt. Boucher buys himself another Brighton house, 1 St.Michael's Place.

A deed of 1903 describes the premises as: 'House on the south side of Victoria Place, known as No: 1 Victoria Place, now occupied by Miss Horsley as a tenant at £40pa rent'. It also describes a passageway on the east side of the house leading to a yard and another building – which has been used as a hall for public meetings. The deed goes on to explain that, as permitted by the charitable trust, this building in the back garden of Victoria House might be used as a Sunday School, Mission Hall or for a charitable purpose in connection with the church of St. Michael. Miss Horsley was either closely connected with the church, or didn't mind Sunday School and other meetings appearing in her back garden on a weekly basis. Perhaps she was the Sunday School teacher for the church.

The Rev. Charles died in 1898, and on the 20th Jan 1903 Victoria House was sold by the Rev. Arthur John Beanlands (presumably the Rev. Charles' son) to charitable trustees. The Rev. Arthur John did not live in the house, but lived in The Rectory, Victoria, BC, Canada and was Canon of the Cathedral Church of Victoria. The charitable trust which then owned the house was not allowed to sell it without permission of the churchwardens of St. Michael's. There is a gap of some four years between the Rev. Charles dying at the end of 1898 and his son selling the house at the beginning of 1903, during which it appears that the church rented the house out to tenants. The final available deed relating to Victoria House is dated 28th July 1928 and records a deed of appointment dated 21st Nov 1910 which replaces the original charitable trustees with a new trust, as legal owners of the house. This new trust was made up of the Chichester Diocesan Fund and Board of Finance (Incorporated) together with the PCC of St. Michael's.

The two churchwardens who were in the new owning trust are named as Harold William Pett and Leonard Whyman Bevan. The deed names the Rev. Herbert Charles Frith, who lived in Windlesham Gardens, as the vicar, but no occupiers or tenants are mentioned. The deed continues to refer to the workshop behind the house as being the parish hall for the church.

Continuing with the churches of the area, the fourth, towards the south-western boundary, was Christ Church, Montpelier Road, consecrated by the Bishop of Chichester on 26th April 1838 and built by Mr. George Cheesman, with George Cheesman junior being the architect. The building is described by Robson and Macdonald (1987) as being a 'rudimentary 13th century Gothic style structure'. It had seating for over 1,000 worshippers, with 620 seats being free, and the first priest-in-charge was the Rev. James Vaughan, who remained there for 43 years. Costing the modest sum of £4,600 in construction, its position might have anticipated souls coming from the later building of that part of the Montpelier estate which was to cover land to the north of Upper North Street. Its early congregation would have come from the seafront homes, the new Temple and Borough Streets, the earlier Chalybeate Street (now Norfolk Road), Montpelier Place, those houses on the south side of what became Upper North Street, and a few years later from the Codrington Estate at the western end of what became the continuation of Western Road. Its interior had

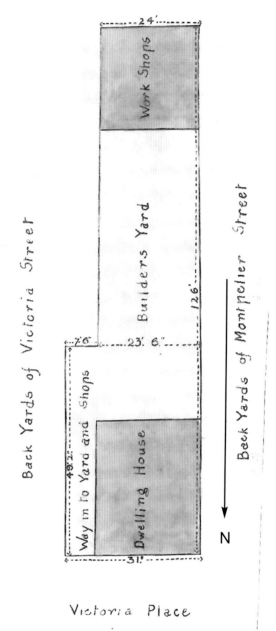

Plan from the 1910 deeds of Victoria House.
From a private collection.

galleries, high pews, a three-decker pulpit and a reredos of The Lord's Prayer, The Creed and The Commandments.

In *The Stranger's Guide* 1855 the Sunday services are listed as 'Morning 11, Afternoon 3.15, Evening 7, Thursday evening at 7'.

Assisting the priest-in-charge was the Rev. A. Turner, curate. Looking at a front view of Brighton's parish church of St. Peter's, Christ Church in Montpelier Road is of a similar, but simplified Gothic Revival design. Of particular interest is the fact that Christ Church had a spire on top of the tower comparable to the one St. Peter's was intended to have, but was never given.

'Christ Church, Montpelier Road, Brighton'.
Coloured line engraving by Rock & Co. Published London, 10th June 1855.
This is another of Rock's illustrated letter papers, similar to the St. Michael and All Angels' print, and is numbered 2797 in Rock's recording system. Rather like Beanlands at St. Michael's, no doubt the Rev. Vaughan also used this image as his letter-heading. The print illustrates the grand terraces that were built either side of the church, probably at the same time, and how similar they were to the later Powis Square design. The terraces further south in this part of Montpelier Road were a little earlier.

The Christ Church spire was modeled on that of Chichester Cathedral, but with a broader base and simpler design than the delicate structure planned for St. Peter's.

Christ Church had a number of schools attached to it. Erredge (1862) notes that adjoining the rear of the church, in Bedford Place, were 'Educational Schools for middle classes, erected in 1843 by Messrs. Wisden and Anscombe'. Presumably this Wisden was one of the family of builders involved in the area's residential development. In addition the church had an infants' school a few yards away in Clarence Gardens.

The only Catholic church in the area is St. Mary Magdalen in Upper North Street, built on the site of a timber merchant's yard during 1861 to 1864 in a decorated Gothic style, with fine stained glass windows. The architect was Gilbert R. Blount (1819–1876). Blount received his early training as a civil engineer under Brunel, working as a superintendent with the Thames Tunnel works. He was later appointed as architect to the Catholic Archbishop of Westminster, Cardinal Wiseman, and his most productive period coincided with a resurgence of Catholic church building in England, which took up much of his career. His preparatory drawings for St. Mary Magdalen's altar and stained glass chancel window are now held in the architectural archives of the University of Pennsylvania. The timber merchant's yard that gave way to St. Mary's was probably that of Henry Tulett, a timber merchant and stonemason

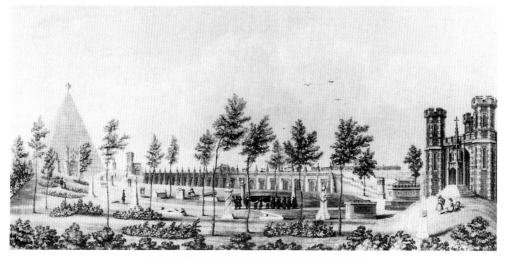

'View of Brighton New Parochial Burial Ground.'
Aquatint by George Earp jnr, published by W.H. Mason c1840.

of 47 Upper North Street at that time. Of the five churches in the area, two lasted a little over a century, Christ Church managed 141 years, and only St. Michael's and St. Mary's remain.

In addition to the local churches, a proposed new burial ground for St. Nicholas' is worth mentioning. A new northern graveyard had been opened on the other side of Church Street in 1824, and this last addition, on the western side of Church Hill, was opened in 1840. The illustration above was published as a proposed design by A.H. Wilds. The large pyramid on the left is taken from a published design of 1825 by Thomas Willson; it was his solution to the burial problems in central London at the time. The idea was that bodies were to be put into long tubes that would then be inserted into the pyramid, and it would have been large enough to take several thousand. The castle entrance to the right was probably inspired by the proposed entrance to London's Kensal Green Cemetery (Ford 1981). Neither was built.

What is still standing today is the Gothic feature wall, built by George Cheesman & Son, and shown in the centre of the print. It still has its thirteen imitation stone relief doorways, with the penultimate doorway on the west being the wooden door into the storerooms behind. Ten years earlier this scene was open downland, and just beyond where the Gothic wall now stands there would have been Clifton Gardens Windmill. By 1851 the Extramural Cemetery on the Lewes Road had been consecrated, so this burial ground was not used after the mid 1850s, and by this date the private gardens to Clifton Terrace had been established on its northern boundary.

4

Vine's Mill

Moving on from the churches in the area, Mr. Vine's cottage, close by his mill, is one of the earliest private dwellings on Church Hill – West Side. The mill itself stood on what is now the corner site of Powis Villas and Powis Grove, according to the archives from the Children's Hospital relating to the Coach House at the top of Clifton Hill.

William Vine (1782–1836) worked a mill in Patcham between 1813 and 1818. On 18th August 1818 he moved to Church Hill and gave his name to Vine Place and the mill. The *Sussex County Magazine* suggests that he had seen the mill advertised for auction on July 20th of that year. In Verrall & Son's auction description the mill was 'lately new and in full trade'. The accompanying dwelling house, now 1 Vine Place and called Rose Cottage today, was included in the sale, but it is not clear whether it was the freehold for sale, or if Vine simply purchased a lease. Lower down the hill, southwards, the Windmill public house was certainly trading in the 1820s (SCM Vol 3) so the present Clifton Place was the direct approach to both Vine's and Clifton Gardens Mill from due south. Simmons, in his extensive unpublished work on windmills, recorded that 'This public house in days gone by stood in open fields, on the old track from St. Nicholas' Church to Hove, now Upper North Street, and was a tiny beer house until it received a full licence in the September of 1828.' Tradition holds that the present snug bar at the back was the early cellar and, as the coldest room, was also used as the local morgue when necessary. By the mid 1840s the undertaker was just around the corner (Thomas Willmot at 12 Victoria Street) and the Windmill Inn landlord at this time was John Pointer. William Vine married Mary Bradford from Eastbourne. A man given to verse, he described his home thus:

"William Vine on the Church Hill
Just by the side of a windmill
The dwelling's neat and fenced around
Its inmates dwell on mercy's ground".
(Finch 2004).

Vine describes his ground as being 'fenced around', and the fence can be seen in the Daniell print illustrated in chapter 11, and in the Bodle painting on a following page. Simmons records that the mill was built towards the end of 1806, probably for a Mr. Weller of Chichester, who only held it for a little while. The only other recorded tenant was a Mr. Wood, who worked it for a short time, but there are no other tenants known up to the auction date. Having bought the mill late in the summer of 1818, Mr. Vine put a notice in the *Sussex Weekly Advertiser* of October 18th 1819 – 'Wanted, a serious man, as a Grinder, who perfectly understands the management of a wind Mill in all its departments'. The *Brighton Herald* of January 19th 1828 reported 'Considerable damage to buildings by a hurricane on Sunday morning. One of the swifts was blown from Mr. Vine's Mill on the Church hill'. That must have been an exciting day for the inmates of the Workhouse – Mr. Vine's windmill sail may well have landed in their grounds.

Henry Bodle, who painted the well-known picture of Vine's Mill (facing page), was a Brighton carpenter and artist, who died in Brighton in 1879. He married William Vine's daughter, Mary on 19 March 1835. In Folthorp's 1864 Directory Henry Bodle is living at 11 Clifton Street, and J. Bodle (connection unknown) is listed at 14 Clifton Street. William Vine had three daughters and one son. After Henry Bodle's death in 1879, his widow Mary, William Vine's daughter, remained in Clifton Street. In the 1881 census she was at 13 Clifton Street along with assorted sons, daughters, in-laws and grandchildren. In that census her occupation is given as 'Income from property', so maybe Henry Bodle had bought a number of houses along Clifton Street.

William Vine was taken seriously ill during 1836 and died that year. He was buried in the family vault in the Hanover Burial Ground. Today William Vine's fifth generation relative is Dr. Stephen Henley, who has done much research on the family. William Vine's third daughter (his youngest) called Esther, married John Henley, a tailor, who was the present Stephen Henley's great-great-grandfather. John & Esther were married on April 18th 1838. He was 28, but Esther is described on the marriage certificate as a minor — she was only 16.

After William Vine's death in 1836, his wife Mary continued to work the mill, with her youngest child and only son James, until about 1842. The 1841 census shows Mary and son James living at 1 Vine Place, together with John Henley and his wife Esther, and their baby Esther Henley. John and Esther were married at Salem Chapel, in Bond Street, Brighton, of which William Vine was a 'devout' member. The Salem Chapel is described as strict Baptist and was first registered for worship in 1837, being demolished in 1974. The *Sussex County Magazine* states that the original building dated from 1787, and after structural alterations William Vine took on his share of work towards the re-opening of the chapel on 21st July 1825.

View of Vine's Mill in 1843
watercolour by Henry Bodle,
now in a private collection in Australia.

The above picture of the mill is the Henry Bodle watercolour, painted in 1843, after William Vine had died, and perhaps it was painted as a keepsake for Vine's widow, once she had sold the business. Edward Cuttress, the Forfars business today, took over the mill from Mrs. Vine in 1842, although in Leppard's 1843 Directory Mary Vine is still listed as the miller in 1 Vine Place. By 1845 Cuttress (but listed as Cutriss) is living in Mary's home, and the mill was finally pulled down sometime during 1849/50. By 1848 the cottage was lived in by Thomas Patching, plumber, painter and glazier, so maybe this was the year that Cuttress stopped using the mill. The whereabouts of this picture of Vine's Mill has remained a mystery for generations, but Stephen Henley has recently traced it to William's great-great-great-grand-daughter, Vine Molony, living in Australia. Mrs. Vine Molony is related to the original miller through two different family lines, due to the marriage of cousins. She herself married an Australian in England, and then emigrated to Australia. The family has five other paintings by Bodle, including a painting of William Vine himself.

In his publication *The Windmills and Millers of Brighton* H.T.Dawes writes 'No building has ever been erected on the site of the old windmill, and it is believed that there is a restrictive covenant in existence to prevent any development'. In fact, the hospital archives show that mill was not where most people assumed it was, in the middle of the hospital staff car park. It was actually nearer the corner of what is now Powis Villas and Powis Grove, and the gardens of the semi-detached houses of 6 and 7 Powis Villas are now where the mill was. The plan from the hospital deeds also shows the track way that became Powis Grove, and the mill workers' cottages were as close to Clifton Gardens Windmill as they were to Vine's Mill. Looking at Bodle's painting, with the view of the sea as it is shown, the artist was standing on the Road to Blatchington, later Clifton Hill, just to the side of where 4 Powis Villas is today. The roofs seen on the left are those of the workers' cottages in Vine Place. The rustic fence to the left of the mill is on the south side of the Blatchington road, (this fence can also be seen in the left foreground of Daniell's print of the Temple in chapter 11), and the wall, lower right in the picture, running back to where Powis Grove is today, is the land division which is the origin of Powis Villas. In the painting this wall appears to be of brick construction. With the line of fencing bottom right, Bodle has portrayed the gentle slope of the land where today Clifton Hill starts descending to the flat plain of downland, where the building of Montpelier Crescent had just begun in the year of the Bodle painting – 1843.

Bodle depicts the lie of the land very well, with the rising slope of Clifton Hill just in front of him, and he seems to have shown how the wide part of the road suddenly becomes the narrow section which passed by the mill before it joined Dyke Road. The width of this narrow part of the road today, beside the flint barn, was originally dictated by the old boundaries of the School House Estate on one side, and Mr. Vine's land on the other. The mill picture pre-dates the naming of Clifton Hill by about three years. Just behind the artist, and to his left, is the home and laundry business of Mrs. Watts, and the rounded flint wall in the left foreground is the south western boundary wall of the school estate. Part of this wall can still be seen on the eastern side of the front garden to 22 Clifton Hill. In the rear garden of this house, in the continuation of this flint wall, there is the remains of a large doorway which must have been an exit from the school grounds onto the open downland of Church Hill. This gateway exit from the school indicates that the flint wall originally encircled the whole school estate, which is how it appears on the following map.

The flint wall and gateway in the rear garden of 22 Clifton Hill. This wall encircled the School House Estate, and the gate would have led out onto the open downland of Church Hill.

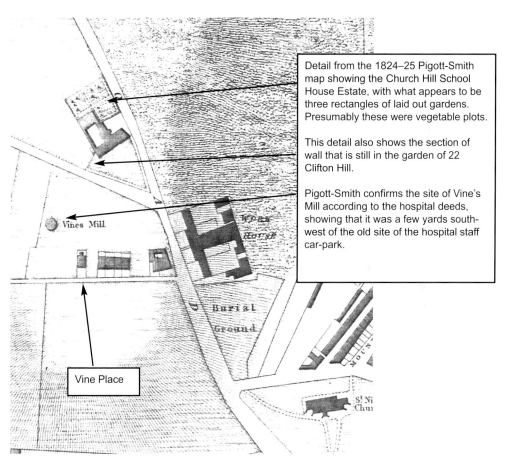

Detail from the 1824–25 Pigott-Smith map showing the Church Hill School House Estate, with what appears to be three rectangles of laid out gardens. Presumably these were vegetable plots.

This detail also shows the section of wall that is still in the garden of 22 Clifton Hill.

Pigott-Smith confirms the site of Vine's Mill according to the hospital deeds, showing that it was a few yards south-west of the old site of the hospital staff car-park.

Vines Mill

Vine Place

There are several oil paintings of Vine's Mill by John Constable, among them 'A Mill near Brighton (Vine's Mill)', which is in the V & A, and 'The Gleaners', painted on August 20th 1824 and said to show Hodson's Mill and Vine's Mill. This painting, illustrated opposite, is in the Tate Gallery, London, and was included in the 'Brighton Revealed' exhibition of 1995. The catalogue entry reads 'The sails depicted seem to be those of Vine's Mill, on the right, and of Hodson's Mill, in the centre. This identification would confirm the inscription on the label attached to this work, which suggests the view is to the north-east.'

However, this description needs reviewing as it is a most unlikely identification for several reasons. First, Hodson's Mill, on a site a few yards to the east of what is now the junction of West Hill Street and West Hill Road, was positioned very close to a line north-east of Vine's Mill. So if Constable had positioned himself looking north-east towards Vine's Mill, Hodson's would have been directly behind it. To see the two mills in the position shown in the painting, the artist would have had to be looking due east, rather than north-east, and standing where Windlesham Road now crosses Windlesham Avenue.

Secondly, not only is that orientation contrary to the label attached to the painting (an unlikely mistake for a landscape painter) but the lie of the land looking from the Windlesham area is completely different from what is seen in the painting, which is the fairly steep southern slope of the south-western part of Church Hill. From the Windlesham area, due east, the land just rises gently to West Hill and the artist would have seen the whole of Hodson's Mill. Even if the artist was further beyond Windlesham, into where York Avenue is now, that would still be true. From that vantage point Constable would also have seen the whole height of Vine's Mill, no part of which would be hidden behind the gently rising ground of the west side of Church Hill.

Thirdly, with the exhibition catalogue description there is the problem of the roof and chimney shown between the mills. From the Windlesham vantage point the land between Hodson's and Vine's mills is that part of Dyke Road from which Albert Road and Alexandra Villas turn off. The only building near that point at that time was the Workhouse, which did not have a chimney on its end gable, and would have stood much higher on the horizon.

The explanation that is more in line with the lie of the land is that the artist is indeed looking north-east, as the label on the painting suggests, but that Hodson's is not one of the mills. During his 1824 visit to Brighton, Constable was staying at Western Cottages, later renamed Sillwood Road, which is just south of Western Road and a little to the east of the junction of Montpelier Road. If the artist had walked from his lodgings straight up the pathway that was to become Hampton Place, and set his easel down as he crossed the track-way that was to become Upper North Street, he would have seen two windmills to the north-east, both partly obscured by the rising land of Church Hill, which is

'The Gleaners, Brighton.' Oil sketch on paper by John Constable, 1824.

as they appear in his painting. He would also have just been able to see the roof of Mr. Vine's cottage between them. But he could not have seen Hodson's Mill which would have been too far beyond the crown of the hill, and in a line directly behind Vine's Mill anyway. So in Constable's sketch, the mill to the left, which he placed in the centre of his composition, would have been Vine's. To the right of that would have been the chimney of Vine's cottage, and the mill on the far right-hand edge of the picture would have been the elusive Clifton Gardens Mill.

As the following paragraphs suggest, this mill is something of an enigma, and this painting by Constable represents its only extant depiction, the other drawing of the mill, mentioned in various histories of windmills, having been lost. Dawes (undated) identifies this Clifton Windmill as a large post-mill with fan-tail gearing, a more modern design than Vine's post-mill, called Clifton Gardens Mill by the end of its life, but not named as such while it was on Church Hill. He suggests John Hilder, of 30 West Street, as the miller. Dawes states that the mill was moved when Hilder died in October 1837 to where Windmill Street is today, at the top of Albion Hill. Because Clifton Gardens Mill does not appear in most of the known maps of this part of Church Hill, the windmill historian H.E.S. Simmons is the principal historical source. He refers to one map drawn by Lieut. R.K. Dawson of the Royal Artillery and dated 1831. This drawing shows a mill near the present Clifton Terrace, with Vine's Mill a short distance further up the hill. The whereabouts of the drawing is not known today, but there are various other references to this mill. On page 93 of the 1924 magazine *The*

Brighton & Hove Archaeologist is written, 'According to the Ordnance Survey Map of 1833 there were two windmills in the vicinity of Powis Square at that time'. Unfortunately, this could also be taken to mean that Powis Square was built by 1833, which of course is not the case. However, as regards the windmills, it can only mean Vine's and Clifton Gardens Mill. The second mention of the Clifton Mill is by F. Bramwell, writing in the *Brighton Herald*. Between the 6th and the 13th August 1938 he wrote a series of articles on 'The Windmills of Brighton' where he claims that it was 'in existence in 1780 and 1806'. Presumably he knew of two such dated references. He describes its location as 150 yards south of Vine's Mill, suggests that Clifton Place was the original approach to it, and that the Windmill Inn took its name from this Clifton Mill, and not from Vine's Mill, as was generally supposed. He names two millers – John Sickelmore in 1800 and W. Hilder in 1822. It was noted earlier that Dawes also mentions Hilder, but calls him John, but there is then a wider discrepancy. Dawes suggests the mill was moved in 1837, but Bramwell's date for the move to the Queens Park area was 1831. This suggests an original hand-written source where the final number is interpreted differently.

The mill is also described in a notice of sale on April 21st 1817 as a 'post mill near Brighton Church, with fan-tail gearing and driving three pairs of stones, being then the property of Mr. W. Murrell, of New England Farm'. Murrell is mentioned in chapter 2 and it is important to note that he was never the owner of Vine's or Hodson's. In Simmons' notes it is described as standing 'in the northwest corner of the present disused burial ground between Clifton Terrace and Upper North Street' and 'on ground now occupied by the gardens of Clifton Terrace'. In fact, the southern boundary of the gardens, and the northern boundary of the burial ground are one and the same place. Simmons goes on to say that by the early 1820s John Hilder had been using it for several years. It is variously referred to as Clifton Windmill or Clifton Gardens Windmill, and is still so named in Kelly's 1855 Directory, by which time it had been sitting atop Albion Hill some eighteen years. However, its name is deceptive.

As 'Clifton' Windmill in the early 1800s it would have been the earliest appearance of that name, pre-dating the naming of Clifton Hill or Terrace by over thirty years. But Simmons puts us straight: '. . . and it should be noted that in connection with this windmill, which seems to have had no particular name, the present street name is used only as a means of identification'. Because the name of 'Clifton' was not used in this area until the latter half of 1845, the strange thing that Simmons seems to be telling us is that while on Church Hill this mill was never named, never called 'Hilder's Mill' for example. Furthermore, it spent eight years on Albion Hill, from 1837 to '45, still with no miller's name attached to it. But it was eventually christened 'Clifton' when the Church Hill roads, the other side of the valley from Albion Hill, were finally given the name of Clifton in 1845. Strange as the delay in naming it may sound, to finally refer to it as Clifton Gardens Windmill is logical in that its original position was where the private gardens to Clifton Terrace were later laid out, and 'Clifton Gardens' was the first identifying name that piece of ground was given in the mid-nineteenth century.

1 Mill Place, originally named Vine Cottage, now called Rose Cottage.
Purchased by William Vine in the summer of 1818, but thought to have been
built some ten years earlier and therefore the oldest private dwelling on
Church Hill – West Side. It still has the roof gable with the chimney stack
that Constable painted. One other house predates Vine Cottage, but
it is on the eastern side of Church Hill. Shelley's (mentioned in chapter 2)
was built in about 1801.

5

Some Land Values

In chapter 1 it was noted that the Kemps re-purchased twenty acres of land on Church Hill in 1817. It was our west side of the sheep down, and they bought it back from the Sackville family for £1,610. Although Yearsley's purchase looked very good value some thirty years later, at the time the widow Kemp and her Trustees may have concluded that £2,100 for just over three acres was a reasonable return, given the economic circumstances. There may have been two reasons for Kemp re-purchasing Church Hill at this time. Within two years of his purchase he was having the Temple built, so plans must have been in mind for that project, and to own the land between his new home and the town itself would have seemed a good idea. The other very likely reason was the land's proximity to the Chalybeate at St. Ann's Well. The spring was visited by the nobility and royalty, and at this early stage Kemp may have envisaged some kind of residential/tourist development for some of these rich visitors to the spring waters. In a Directory of 1800 Brighton described itself as 'one of the most fashionable towns in England' and the best in 'accommodating its visitors in everything which can contribute to their health, their comfort and their amusement'. The few rich landowners obviously considered how best to capitalize on the enviable reputation the town had.

If Kemp had entertained thoughts of the development of Church Hill, between his home and St. Nicholas' Church, from which the gentry could visit the spring waters, the building of the Workhouse in 1821/2 would have seen an end to any such plans. But it seems such ideas were in his mind to the west of his Church Hill land. By 1823 Kemp Town was underway, and encouraged by the prospect of financial success, in 1825 Kemp and one of his Baring brothers-in-law entered into a contract with the Rev. Thomas Scutt to purchase much of the Wick Estate. Payment was due in 1829, obviously with the expectation that Kemp Town had returned good profits by then. The Scutt family had owned the undeveloped land of The Wick and the Brunswick Estates for several generations, which land included the mineral spring, and their plans, with C.A. Busby, to build houses for the gentry and the middle classes were already materializing – Brunswick Square and Terrace had been started in 1824. Kemp was to buy all that land which Scutt had not yet assigned to individual developers, plus all the grazing land around Wick House, together with the Chalybeate (note 2). The Brunswick development was only about one tenth of the total purchase, and when the plans were exhibited at the Royal Academy in 1825 some of the land was described as Scutt's and some as the property of Kemp, (Dale 1947). As security for the 1829 payment Scutt was given seven houses in Kemp Town. But by 1830 financial problems had forced Kemp to sell his interest in Wick to Sir Isaac Lyon Goldsmid for just over £55,000, which money was paid direct to Scutt. The Rev. Scutt's father, also called Thomas, had developed the southern part of the Wick Estate, the present sites of Brunswick Square and Adelaide Crescent, into a centre for brick-making during the early eighteenth century. By 1722 he was supplying the bricks for the building of Stanmer House, (Beswick 1993).

This date of 1830, when Kemp gives up his plans for Wick, is relevant to the development of our area. It seems to mark the beginning of Kemp's financial problems, and June 1830 in the deeds to 88 Upper North Street is the earliest date found of Kemp selling small pieces of land on Church Hill – West side. These deeds to 88 Upper North Street refer to an agreement of June 15/16th 1830, by which Kemp sold a tract of land on West Hill, on the north side of what was then called North Street Road, to William and Francis Hallett. This tract of land included the plot for number 88, which house was built by William Hallett, who sold it on in 1837 to Edward Vallance for £285. Unfortunately no sale price from Kemp was mentioned in this deed.

William Hallett was a figure of growing importance in Brighton at this time, as well as being an influential developer on the lower slopes of Church Hill – West Side. He was born in Rotherfield, 10th April 1794, and was in Brighton by 1811, working as a carpenter on the Pavilion. By 1825 he is recorded as having 150 men working on his building enterprises. He became the second mayor in 1855, after Lt. Col John Fawsett (Dale 1976) and was also appointed chief magistrate that year, then again in 1866/67 (Martin 1871). In the 1860s he was one of the twelve Aldermen of the town. He built St. John the Baptist RC church in Bristol Road, and the Bristol Hotel c1835, of which he was the proprietor, in Marine Parade (now Bristol Court). He also founded the Kemp Town Brewery and built some of the houses in Kemp Town, notably numbers 19 and 20 Sussex Square for the Marquess of Bristol. In 1849 he was on a sub-committee which managed Brighton races. At that time he owned much land in and around the racecourse, as well as some three hundred acres of farmland, including New England as mentioned in chapter 2, and various inns (Note 3). His eldest son, who took over the Kemp Town Brewery, was also called William.

In Chapter 2 Kemp's early sales are mentioned – the November 1834 sale of two plots in Victoria Road and the 1835 Kemp/Hallett lease agreement on 16 parcels of land in Upper North Street. Money problems for the gentry were an opportunity that the builders and tradesmen of Brighton grabbed with both hands. Kemp had not managed his development of Kemp Town with a sensible economic plan. Instead of building a small part and selling that before building more, as the Rev. Scutt had been doing to the west, Kemp attempted to build a great many of the facades in one go. This would have made the economics difficult in the best of times, but with bank failures and city companies going under in the recession, his project was probably doomed from its early days. Add to this the fact that the recession particularly affected the monied classes (precisely those to whom he needed to sell Kemp Town), much more than it affected the small local businessmen like John Yearsley.

It is understandable why his widow, a few years later, was the keen seller, and why the Yearsleys and Halletts and Wisdens of Brighton were in the market to buy. It might also have been the case that, after Kemp's death, members of the Baring family, undoubtedly suffering the effects of the recession themselves, were pressing Mrs. Kemp to repay the large sums of money that her husband had borrowed from them over the years. Regarding his bad financial plans for the development of east Brighton, it is only for us in the twenty-first century to be thankful that Kemp set out to build everything in one go. Had he not done so, we might not have Sussex Square and Lewes Crescent as they are today.

At the top of Church Hill the scene that emerges for the mid-to-late 1840s is of the very busy widow Kemp and her late husband's brothers-in-law, the Baring brothers, part selling and part developing Church Hill – West Side, with considerable involvement from the Faithfull family as well as John Yearsley, the Halletts and other local builders. It is assumed that the septet mentioned in chapter 2 went on to develop the whole of Clifton Terrace, and that it was Baring money, and possibly some from Henry and George Faithfull, that financed the facades of these houses. David Beevers, in correspondence about Clifton Terrace in 1997, writes '. . there was obviously a controlling influence over the elevations of the (Clifton) terraces and I would suggest that this came from the Baring family'.

The second Mrs. Kemp was a wealthy lady when she married, (she was the widow of Vigors Harvey of Killiane Castle, Co. Wexford) but it is difficult to imagine that she remained uninvolved in her late husband's financial problems, and by the mid 1840s she was in the necessary process of selling some assets, to fund the development of others. After her husband's death in France she came back to Brighton in April 1846 and within a few months had started her negotiations with Yearsley. Mrs. Kemp died on 28th March 1860 in Tunbridge Wells.

The relatively low price of £2,100 for John Yearsley's freehold payment does need some explaining. In 1834 Kemp sold a plot 68 by 73 feet for £205, but by 1849 it seems that his widow was only able to command £2,100 for just under three acres. At this stage it is worth looking at the social position of Church Hill. Carder (1990) suggests the first houses on the east side of Clifton Road were started c1830 (fifteen years earlier than this research suggests), these being the three-storey homes on the east side, and he then suggests c1850 for the building of the Italianate villas in Clifton Hill, numbers 1 to 4. The Crescent Inn, owned by Thomas Curtis, and the livery stables in Clifton Mews were developed around this time, being the next features on the road to Blatchington that have mention in the directories after Mrs. Watts' laundry service. In the 1846 street Directory there are no numbers in Clifton Hill and the listing reads 'Curtis, Charles, Crescent Inn, Killner, James Wheelwright, Tyler, James Esq.' In 1848, still without numbers, J. Taylor is listed in the livery stables, Clifton-mews, and by 1862 Mr. Taylor is entered as 'postmaster, private and livery stables, Clifton mews'. He obviously had an eye to developing his business as opportunities arose.

Just before this development of Church Hill was starting to take shape, the year of 1841 saw the most socially divisive influence on any established town, the building of the railway terminus. Once a railway terminus was positioned in a town, you only lived down wind of it if you had to and could afford nothing else. Church Hill was up-wind of the trains, looked down over the town and in the early Victorian period became, in Geoffrey Mead's words, the 'West End' of town. However, the suggested sale price of the undeveloped land to Yearsley seems very depressed, despite the fact that it was in this desirable position in relation to the new terminus. In 1834, before the trains came, Kemp sold 550 square yards for £205. On a pro rata valuation for just under three acres sold in 1849, Yearsley should have paid over £6,000, yet the price was a little over a third of that, which lends weight to the idea of Kemp's widow being in the difficult position of a fairly keen seller. The price of £3,847 that Thomas Wisden had paid Budgen's executors for a similar piece of land on the northern side of Clifton Hill in 1843 (mentioned in detail in chapter 6) also seems quite low compared with individual plots that Kemp had sold earlier.

The recession that followed the Napoleonic war, and the Stock Exchange crisis of 1825, which would have made selling large houses in Kemp Town difficult, was still having a depressing effect on business when Kemp sold his plot in Victoria Road in 1834. By the time his widow was selling, the economic situation was only a little better, and large tracts of land would certainly have been more difficult to sell than small plots. The low price is not surprising given the depth of the December 1825 stock market crash and the resulting financial depression that affected the monied classes. The other depressing influence was that most of the land was overlooked by the Workhouse and Infirmary. This institution would have increased its number of inmates and its general activity in the area considerably in the 25 years between being built and the selling of Church Hill.

The stock exchange problems of 1825 represented the first major banking crisis in England. The Government and the Bank of England had worked together on reflationary measures from 1822, but the boom and balance of trade problems by 1824–25 had resulted in a sharp reduction in the Bank's gold reserves. Considerable assets were tied up abroad, particularly in mining and agricultural ventures and loans to the newly independent countries of South America. Alarm bells started ringing with a crisis in the cotton trade in the August of 1825. Three London banks stopped payments, other banks were seriously affected and by December there was financial panic in London and other cities. Many brokers in the City went bankrupt as South American governments defaulted on their loans. Between July 1825 and June 1826 there were 60 bank failures. Many politicians and society figures were left exposed. Lord Palmerston is said to have lost his chance of becoming chancellor, while the young Benjamin Disraeli and the novelist Sir Walter Scott were among those who spent the rest of their lives paying off their resulting debts.

The fluctuation in Brighton's population growth echoes the Stock Exchange recession. Fleet (1847) gives an interesting record of the town's development over three decades. In 1811 he records a population of 12,012 souls with 2,077 houses. By 1821 there has been an increase in the population of a hundred per cent to 24,429, with 3,947 houses. Up to 1831 the increase slows to 70 per cent, with 40,634 souls in 7,700 houses, and from 1832 to 1841 the growth is down to just 25 per cent. It is in this final decade that Kemp struggled to sell large houses in Kemp Town, he also started selling Church Hill, and in 1837 fled from his creditors to France.

There was a variety of lucky circumstances which came together in the mid-nineteenth century and enabled a relatively new social group to build the first Victorian middle-class residential development of central Brighton. First, the trains arrived and brought new trade and business to the town. Secondly, the country was emerging from the recession which had caused a downturn in the fortunes of the 'old money' landowners, whereas the local tradesmen, businessmen and builders were experiencing an upturn in their fortunes and their confidence.

The decade to 1841 was the period of lowest growth in nineteenth century Brighton, but from then on the trains, the connection to London, the demand for middle-class housing and the increase in business activity developed a great momentum in the town. There was the fresh excitement that Regency architecture, with its new look and new materials, gave to the builders and architects of the town, and finally the career of Amon Henry Wilds was entering its most inspired period.

Dr. Russell built the first, more modest, twin-gabled house that was illustrated in chapter 1, around the spring that became St. Ann's Well, and it was replaced by the classical building below in about 1830. In Wallis it is described as 'A commodious and elegant building, comprising a reading room and other conveniences'. It was demolished in 1934. It is most likely that some of the fashionable people visiting the chalybeate stayed with Kemp at the Temple, just five minutes walk away, as they would also have stayed with Sir Isaac Goldsmid at Wick Hall.

'The Chalybeate.'
Lithograph c1830 by E.Taylor, 95 Western Road, published with the title 'Brighton Chalybeate' then republished in Wallis's Royal Edition 'Brighton As It Is', 1836. under the above title.

John Yearsley's home, Grove House, 4 Powis Villas, in 2007.
Under its original name, Grove Villa was owned by members of the Yearsley family from when it was built in 1849 until January 1920.

6

The Builders Move In

Quite a few names are associated with the development on the north side of Clifton Hill, and unlike the more cohesive structure of the Powis estate, the variety of styles illustrates the variety of developers. Carder suggests that the first homes on Clifton Hill were the four semi-detached Italianate villas on the western end, looking south. These homes are similar in style to 5 Powis Villas. Moving eastwards across Clifton Road from the Crescent public house there is one 'link-detached' house, number 7, which was originally called Clifton Villa: this was Yearsley's home until he had his new house built in Powis Villas. Moving up the hill on the north side there are three different building lines for three separate terraces, two of just two houses each, and then the group from number 15 to 22. All this is on the north side, and much information has come from the deeds of houses on this side of Clifton Hill.

John Yearsley's first home in the Powis area, Clifton Villa – detail from the c1845 engraving of Montpelier Crescent

The house in 2007

Concerning the four Italianate semi-detached villas just mentioned, numbers 1 to 4 Clifton Hill, number 3 has some useful documents. There is a copy of an agreement of 24th December 1849 regarding a piece of land at the back of the southernmost house of Montpelier Crescent (i.e. the land for 3 & 4 Clifton Hill) between Edward Bruton, stonemason of Brighton, with Henry Faithfull and Thomas Wisden, builder of Henfield and Brighton, and Frederick Cooper, gentleman. This is the piece of land for the two semi-detached homes, numbers 3 and 4, which can now be dated to c1850. This makes them a few years later than some of the terraced houses further up the hill on this north side of the road. However, Folthorp's Directory for Clifton Hill in 1848 starts by listing Miss Copeman, Langley Villa, and Mrs.J. Rycroft Best at Bilham Villa. The entry then goes straight to the Crescent Inn. So these two named villas must be numbers 1 and 2 Clifton Hill, built some two or three years before numbers 3 and 4. Judging by their appearance the same developers were involved, although the second pair never had the Italianate towers of numbers 1 & 2. Professor David Robson feels these four homes are probably A.H. Wilds' work, and comments that they can be looked upon as Brighton's prototype semi-detached house, satisfying the image needs of the well-off middle class family. However, it seems strange that if Thomas Wisden was the builder involved in the purchase of the land he did not then actually build them, so maybe Wisden simply referred to a Wilds' architectural publication for the design of the houses. This seems a reasonable assumption bearing in mind the date of December 1849. Wilds was 65 years old, and earlier that year he had started work on the most ambitious scheme of his long career, the horseshoe arrangement of the 48 houses of Park Crescent. With such an undertaking in hand, would he really have come back up Church Hill for four relatively small houses that were not part of a coherent development plan? Wisden himself appears as a very busy independent builder of considerable means, with no indication that he was used by Wilds on particular projects.

Still with the documents to 3 Clifton Hill, John Yearsley is involved again. The deeds tell us that houses on the eastern border of this land are referred to as the property of Yearsley. At present it is difficult to understand the plural, 'houses', as only number 5 is available before the Crescent Inn, number 6. In the street guides for 5 Clifton Hill the occupant is the builder George Maynard by 1856, and by the late 1860s it is Mrs. Palmer's lodging house. This property is now the taxi garage, but it could certainly have been two semi-detached homes, although with the inn numbered 6 this does seem unlikely. Also documented at number 3 is a covenant, drawn up between Yearsley and Thomas Wisden, whereby Bruton had to build a house to the value of at least £250. This would have been number 5, which presumably Bruton had agreed to pay Wisden to build, before buying both land and new house from Yearsley.

Bruton's involvement is interesting here, as he was a stonemason, and some of the skirting boards and the staircases in these houses were made in marble and stone, rather than the usual timber. Opposite these homes is 37 Clifton Hill, the only house which is not part of the end-buildings of the larger terraces of Powis Road and St. Michael's Place that make up this lower section of the road on the south side. It is one of the pair of what were originally built as semi-detached houses, with its sister house round the corner fronting onto Powis Road. They were built before the taller terraces so brutally swamped them, and the one in Powis Road today was obviously part of Clifton Hill originally, as it does not feature in the early street directory entries for Powis Road.

It was noted earlier that Kemp had mortgaged part of his Church Hill land to Thomas Budgen's executors in 1832 (the year of Kemp's second marriage). This was the triangular piece of land bounded by what is now Dyke Road, Montpelier Crescent, and Clifton Hill. It represents all that land directly north of Yearsley's later purchase and therefore all the land on the north side of Clifton Hill. This gives an explanation of why, in his will of 1835, Kemp leaves land on the south side of the 'Road to Blatchington' to his son, but land on the north side of the road is not included – it was no longer free. The mortgage on this land included the usual power of sale, which was exercised by Thomas Budgen the son and one of his father's executors, in 1843. The buyer was Thomas Wisden, the Brighton builder, who paid £3,847. 10s and who immediately sold on the south-eastern portion to the Rev. William Henry Butler, who, prior to this, had leased the site from Kemp for his school building.

While looking at the north side of Clifton Hill, the deeds to number 20 mention the land demised by T.R. Kemp to the executors of Thomas Budgen by way of the above mentioned 1832 mortgage with power of sale. An indenture dated 13th October 1845 gives us the parties involved with the site for number 20: on one side W.H. Smithers (note 4), gent of Sussex and later mayor of Brighton and resident of the Gothic House on Western Road, Ben Laker, boot and shoe-maker of Brighton, and James Tyler, bookseller (who later lived in the house); and on the other side William Watts – laundryman, Thomas Watts – tailor, William Pierson – butterman, and James Waller – grocer in Brighton. By a deed dated 6th Jan 1846 Ben Laker bought the piece of land for number 20 from Smithers for £74. 9. 0d, referred to in the deed of Jan 26th. This deed of 26th Jan 1846 confirms that William Heaves Smithers sold to Benjamin Laker a piece of land in Clifton Hill. There is no house at this stage: the deeds make an interesting reference to 'a piece of land now stumped out' and mention restrictions on the use of the land. Once the house was built, Laker sold it to Tyler, who became its first occupant. Here can be seen the development of this familiar process of pairs and trios of traders and small businessmen, gaining or granting each other mortgages as necessary, buying a large parcel of land, and carving it up between themselves as the homes are built. This deed talks about the road leading from 'the Montpellier Road to the Workhouse', then adds 'now called Clifton Hill'. The piece of land was 112 foot by 19 foot. The house was numbered 20 by 1866 and named Clifton Cottage. To the north it was abutting the land of the Rev. Dr. William Henry Butler's School House Estate, on the west the land of James Tyler, on the east the land of Thomas Watts. The Rev. Butler's land obviously extended behind the gardens of numbers 20 to 22. The price of £74 in 1846 for land that amounted to 230 square yards seems to indicate that the arrival of the railway did not have an immediate effect on prices in the area. In 1834 Kemp had sold 550 square yards for £205, a slightly more expensive deal.

From the sales by the Budgens, smaller parcels of this large tract of land were then owned by Thomas Wisden, builder, the Rev. Butler and William Thomas Watts, laundryman. This Thomas Wisden is also listed in this 1843 Directory as a brickmaker based in Hove and as a builder at 15 Hampton Place, while in the deeds of 3 Clifton Hill, dated 1849, he is introduced as being from Henfield. Apart from his obvious influence in the Clifton area, by the mid 1840s Wisden had quite a varied property portfolio around the town. In 1845 he is listed as owning and renting out 30 and 31 Montpelier Road; he was the landlord of 113 Western Road, numbers 24 and 25 Norfolk Road and 12 Sillwood Place; and he also owned a shop and a yard at 10 Hampton Street (ESRO BH/B/4/36b/2 and BH/B/4/35/2).

The first deeds to 7 Clifton Hill, on the corner of Clifton Road, are dated 29th March 1845. The parties mentioned are William Watts – laundryman, John Yearsley – ironmonger, James Waller – grocer, William Pierson – butterman, Thomas Wisden – builder, John Budgen of Frant in Sussex, gentleman, the Rev. William Henry Butler, John Lewis – Brighton timber merchant and Thomas Watts of Brighton. The deed starts by citing two agreements of 17th May 1843 in which Budgen, Wisden and Butler sell a piece of land. William Watts is the buyer, and he is acting with T. Watts and J. Waller. W. Watts bought the land for £600 and had a mortgage for that sum with W. Pierson. The second referred-to agreement of this date of May 1843 is from Pierson, allowing Watts to sell off a part of his mortgaged land to John Yearsley, and this is that piece of land which is now covered by numbers 7, 8, & 9 Clifton Hill. Yearsley then appointed John Lewis as a trustee of his property, presumably to protect his young children's inheritance as this was the new family home, and through the summer of 1845 John Yearsley had built for himself, most likely by Wisden again, 7 Clifton Hill, with gardens extending some fifty feet on its eastern side, up the slope of Clifton Hill.

At this time it is not called Clifton Hill, but is referred to as the road leading from the 'New Road' (later Clifton Road), to the Poor House. This enables us to put the naming of the road as Clifton Hill some time between March 1845 and the publication of the 1846 Street Directory, where Clifton Hill is first listed. Unfortunately these street directories are not dated with a month, but a few of them promise to be correct at a particular time of the year – for example 1856 promises to be accurate to September of that year, 1862 promises May, and so on. Unfortunately the 1846 Directory gives no such clue, so from the street directories it appears that Clifton Hill was christened after March 1845 and, from the deeds to number 20 already mentioned, before 6th January of 1846. From the Montpelier Crescent print illustrated in chapter 8 we know that Clifton Villa pre-dated the Crescent Inn, possibly by less than twelve months, but the 1846 Directory omits Yearsley's new house, concentrating as it does on the appearance of the inn and the increased business activities of the Mews. Missing new houses that are built during the compiling of a new directory is not particularly uncommon. The building of the inn would have been the most important observation, and there would have been the added confusion of the naming of Clifton Hill during the editing of the directory. With such a pace of development around the town, the work of compiling accurate street directories must have been beset with problems.

Returning to the March 1845 deed, it has a memorandum, dated 28th May 1851, noting that John Yearsley had sold a smaller part of his original purchase from W. Watts, the land for number 7, to Thomas Young, the builder. This smaller piece of land now represents 8 and 9 Clifton Hill, but it was originally the gardens to Yearsley's home at number 7. The other parties mentioned in this memorandum are trustees of the Brighton & Hove Benefit Building Society: George Dempster – a Brighton solicitor and town commissioner – Richard Green – ironmonger, William Catt esq. and Thomas Isaacson – brewer and town commissioner.

The sale of the eastern end of this piece of land explains why Clifton Villa, number 7 Clifton Hill, now seems so inappropriately positioned within its land, leaving little room for gardens on any of its three sides, and why it looks as if it was built as a detached house although it is now actually attached to the end of a short terrace. And while the two houses built in Yearsley's garden are very different from number 7, the original dwarf garden wall that surrounded Yearsley's house continues in front of them. Folthorp's Street Directory indicates a Mr. Charles Manders living in Clifton Villa in 1850. Taylor's Directory then tells us that Miss Oxenden was the occupant by 1854. It is not known if Mr. Manders purchased the house, without its gardens, from Yearsley, or simply rented it. On 26th July 1859 William Watts sold another plot, again just a part of his larger purchase within this original triangle of land, with an 18ft frontage on to Clifton Hill, to William Baker, china dealer of Brighton, for £150. This plot represents the present number 16 Clifton Hill, and the deeds to that house mention that it lay immediately west of a similar plot, the present number 17, which had been sold to Baker in 1855, and on which a dwelling had been built.

The houses 8 and 9 Clifton Hill, now standing on the original garden of Clifton Villa, the corner property to Clifton Hill and Clifton Road.

The owners of number 9 Clifton Hill have deeds which refer to an agreement dated 28th May 1851, the date of the memorandum on number 7's deeds just mentioned, and this tells us that during 1851 Thomas Young was building numbers 8 and 9 Clifton Hill 'at his own expense'. These deeds also show that William Watts owned number 10 Clifton Hill in 1872. The name of William Watts appears again later, in partnership with John Yearsley, and in connection with the first houses to be built in Clifton Road. So, from the mortgage sale of 1843 by Thomas Budgen, the various buyers involved purchased a parcel of land and then often sold part of their purchase on: William Watts sold sections of land on to Yearsley and later to William Baker, and Yearsley sold part of his purchase to Thomas Young.

On this northern side of Clifton Hill, a fascinating story with a royal connection was published in the local press on 14th August 1862. The King of Dahomey, West Coast of Africa, was very involved in the slave trade as well as human ritual sacrifice. Capt. Frederick Forbes RN was sent in his vessel 'Bonetta' to negotiate an end to these practices. The captain got on very well with the 'slaying monarch', and the king bestowed on Forbes the gift of a little negro girl. After he brought the child back to England, Queen Victoria agreed to make arrangements for her care and education. She was christened Sarah Forbes Bonetta (known as Sally), and to safeguard her health the Queen sent her back to Africa for the rest of her childhood, bringing her back to England to finish her education – and this is when the story comes to Brighton. The Queen selected Mrs. Welsh of 17 Clifton Hill, who a local newspaper described as a 'lady of high connections and position', to complete Miss Bonetta's social education and oversee her introduction to society. The article then extols her general standing and ability, and reports 'such was the girl who has for some time past been residing with Mr. & Mrs. Welsh in Brighton'. The ESRO has details of her marriage to a 33-year-old merchant from Lagos called James Pinson Davies – a widower. Mr. Davies was living at 9 Victoria Road, and Sally

Forbes Bonetta was still living at 17 Clifton Hill – noted in Folthorpe's 1862 street Directory as Belmont Cottage, the home of Miss Welsh. The marriage was at St. Nicholas' on 14th Aug. 1862 – the date of the article. Capt. Forbes' journal entry on the gift of the child was in 1850, and he thought the child about 8 years old, so she married at about twenty years of age. By the time of the marriage Capt. Forbes had died, so his father gave Sally away. The newly-weds left for Sierra Leone, and in 1867 Sally returned to Windsor to present her new daughter, Victoria, to the Queen, who became the new child's godmother. Sally and her daughter visited again in 1873. Then in 1880, Queen Victoria's diary entry reads: 'August 24th – Victoria has just learned of her mother's death at Madeira'. Victoria was in England at the time of the news and Madeira was on the route from Lagos to London. Sally had died of consumption. The Queen decided to give Victoria an annuity, and she also paid for her to go to Cheltenham Ladies College: she started there in 1881.

Returning to the north side of Clifton Hill, there is another, earlier instance of the name of Watts, laundry owner, who is previously mentioned. In Leppard's Directory of 1839 there is a page advertisement for Mrs. Watts - Laundress and Clear Starcher at 'Lone Cottage, Top of Montpelier Road'. She recommends herself to the gentry and claims large areas of open fields for drying. The picture illustrating her advertisement (in chapter 8) is rather misleading. It is not clear whether she means the top of the road where it meets Dyke Road or that part of Montpelier Road where it reaches the top of the hill and meets the road to Blatchington (Clifton Hill). However, Folthorp's 1850 Directory answers that question – under the entry for Clifton Hill is listed C. Thomas, dairyman, Lone Cottage. This, together with evidence from the 1851 census papers, firmly establishes Lone Cottage as a building on Clifton Hill. The Watts family of 'laundresses and clear starchers' in this area is a little complicated. Under this trade heading in 1843 is Mary Watts, Vine Place, Church-hill. In 1846 there was Mrs. Elizabeth Watts & Daughter, 'proprietors of extensive drying grounds, top of Montpelier Road'. With this particular description of the drying grounds this sounds like the Mrs. Watts of the 1839 Leppard's advertisement, who, having been joined in business by her daughter by 1846, has sold the premises to the dairyman, Mr. Thomas, by 1850. More research into the premises known as Lone Cottage is discussed in chapter 8.

Although it is not clear in the 1848 Directory, Folthorp's 1850 volume lists 'Clifton Road – leading from Victoria Road to Dyke Road'. It then lists Powis Place (now Square) as 'first right in Clifton Road from Victoria Road'. This indicates that what is now known as Powis Road was seen as part of Clifton Road at that time. This pre-dates the houses on the west side of the present Powis Road.

In the following view of the Temple, Church Hill with cattle and sheep grazing on it is shown rising on the left, and we are viewing its northern slopes as it climbs to the highest point where Albert Road and the Children's Hospital are later built. In the distance, to the right of the Temple, are the gardens laid out around the chalybeate spring, with the plantation of firs on its far side. The flat plain of open downland in the centre is now Montpelier Crescent, Denmark Terrace and part of Clifton Road, while the Road to Blatchington, later Clifton Hill, runs just the far side of the hill. These flat fields were also used as the Temple Fields Cricket Ground, mentioned in chapter 8. Once the railway arrives Buckingham Place will skirt around this side of the hill before descending to the station: the Road to Steyning, now Dyke Road, is unseen in the dip of the landscape behind the hill. The artist was standing on the highest point where Howard Place is now, before the railway cutting was dug, and the figures by the fencing in the foreground are close to where Buckingham Place now runs. Within thirty years of this engraving all this open space was covered in housing and the view no longer existed. Of the six known views of the Temple, this one and 'Ovington Near Brighton' by Daniell, when viewed together, give the most comprehensive illustration of Church Hill during the 1820s.

'The Temple, the seat of T.R.Kemp Esqr.'
Aquatint engraving from C. & R. Sickelmore's "Select Views of Brighton", c1827.

Daniell shows us the western slopes where Clifton Hill and the Powis Estate were to be built, while Sickelmore depicts the descent of the northern slope where Compton Avenue and West Hill Street now stand, and the flat plain awaiting all the routes that lead up to and away from the Seven Dials. The Dials junction, and later the roundabout itself, was to be built on the far right of the picture, in that small triangle of field which is fenced around.

Detail of 'The Temple Grammar School' from Horsfield's *History of Sussex*.
Line engraving by H. Ogg after a drawing by G.Earpe, published 1835.

The two previous prints of the Temple show the addition to the top floor of the building and the new chimneys. The original design of the Temple, without the four high chimneys, is shown in the Daniell print titled 'Ovington' in chapter 11. The Temple Grammar School engraving (detail above and illustrated in full in chapter 7) also shows the Antheum, which had in fact collapsed in August 1833. Just to the left of the Temple is a simplified depiction of Sir Isaac Lyon Goldsmid's Wick Hall, only a couple of years old at this stage. This is the only known nineteenth century view of Goldsmid's home. The artist of the above engraving is standing on Dyke Road, more or less where West Hill Road was later built, and this scene illustrates the amazing spectacle on view to the inmates of the Workhouse. Other aspects of this interesting engraving are discussed in chapter 7. The plans for creating West Hill Road itself, together with Guildford Road, were submitted for approval by Mr. Donne on 3rd February 1849 (ESRO DB/D6/14). While no horse drawn vehicles could have negotiated the incline of Guildford Road, the pathway was already in use as a convenient pedestrian access between the new station and the Church Hill development. The route can be seen in the Nibbs lithograph in chapter 2, where figures are walking beside the flint wall that borders the northern edge of the Workhouse grounds.

Some of the houses in Folthorp's 1850 list for Clifton Road are named. Numbers 1 and 2 both seem to be called Warwick Villa, Down Villa is number 3,

6 is called South Down Villa, 7 is Douro Villa, then 9 is Eagle Villa and 12½ is Sandford Lodge. Only one of these houses is identifiable by name today – as you walk along the present Clifton Road no house names are left, but 9 has the word 'villa' above the front porch, and above that is a large stone model of an eagle – Eagle Villa. Presumably number 7, Douro Villa, was so named in memory of the Duke of Wellington's eldest son. In the 1854 rate book (ESRO BH/B/4/37/2) numbers 46 to 53 (now in Compton Avenue) are listed as 'house, lecture room, playground and buildings'. The Rev. Coombes, the vicar of All Saints', lived at 62.

On the south side of Clifton Hill, on Yearsley's major land purchase, the first homes after Lone Cottage on the north side, appear to be the line of four small Regency style houses beside Grove Villa. The deeds to one of these, number 24, give us some details of their origins. There is a copy of an 1837 agreement between T.R.Kemp (this is the year he went to France) and Charlotte Norton regarding what was then agricultural land: it is dealing in 'pauls of land' and refers to the land in the name of 'Beaches'. There is a deed of 15th April 1847 between George Faithfull and John Yearsley on the one hand, and Fred White (the chemist further down the road) and William John Faithfull, where Fred White has leased the plot of land from Yearsley and erected a house, then referred to as 10 Clifton Hill. In a deed of 1st October 1847 Fred White grants a six year sub-lease on number 10 to the Rev. Robert Winter. Yearsley granting a lease on the land for these houses ties in with his original agreement with Mrs. Kemp dated September 1846, which was leasehold. He did not buy the freehold until the spring of 1849. The next deed with number 24, of 22nd November 1864, refers to the house that was known as 10 Clifton Hill, but which is now identified as number 24 (its modern day number) as still being on a monthly lease to William E. Winter.

The rest of this middle part of the south side of Clifton Hill was made up of land which was the rear gardens of houses in Powis Square, as shown on the map later in this chapter. This land was developed with three terraced houses in 1964. Then the few shops, with accommodation over, form the curved corner site leading round to Powis Square. In Taylor's 1854 Directory the shops were a bookseller and wool shop, Fred Wright's chemist and tobacconist, a greengrocer and Mrs. Russell, laundress. The western end on the south side of Clifton Hill is made up of the end buildings of Denmark Terrace and St. Michael's Place, and these stand just west of Yearsley's original purchase.

Some deductions about this part of the development come from the engraving of St. Michael's Church illustrated in chapter 3. The church was built in 1861-62, and St. Michael's Place did not exist before the parish church from which it took its name. But in the engraving of the church, dated 1866, the back of house number 8 on the west side of Powis Road is clearly shown, and the engraver has portrayed tall shadows on the back of this Powis Road house, supposedly cast by the east side terrace of St. Michael's Place. Because of the east-west orientation of the church, the shadows in the print could never have actually been in the direction shown. The artist obviously had a preliminary sketch to engrave from. He put shadows in place when back in his London workshop and assumed that St. Michael's Place would have cast a shadow over the southern most Powis Road house, but of course the shadows don't fall that way. So the engraving of the church suggests St. Michael's Place was casting its shadow over Powis Road in 1866, but apart from the sun's incorrect position, the image is a little premature anyway. In the Index of New Street Plans (ESRO DB/D6/14) the proposal for this new road was presented to Brighton Town Council by a Mr. Simpson on 24th March 1863. The actual drawn plan for the road, named as St. Michael's Place and then, in brackets, (Trocke's Field), was given on 3rd December of that year, but the detailed building plans were not submitted until 15th January 1868, nearly five years after the initial proposal and two years after the engraving was published. The first printed listing is in Page's 1868 Directory, and at that date only two houses are sold and occupied. 1 St. Michael's Place is owned by the Misses Peele, and 2 is the new home of F.G. Tippett Esq. The 1869 listing still has only the first three houses occupied, and interestingly the Misses Peele have sold to Capt. Boucher, who three years earlier had sold Victoria House to the vicar of St. Michael's church.

It is not until the early 1870s that St. Michael's Place becomes fully occupied, with several numbers listed as 'a furnished house', to be let to visitors. Professor Robson points out that St. Michael's Place is identical to many of the terraces around Paddington, London, and with six floors to each house on the west side, and five floors each on the east, it is probably the highest density Victorian housing in central Brighton, hence the length of time it took to build. This increase in housing density in our area, as an estate is being developed, happens today. The first flats and houses in Brighton Marina were given far more space than the later ones, and so Powis/Clifton goes from the detached houses of Powis Villas to one of the most densely packed streets in the centre of town, and illustrates how the demand for large middle class homes in the Church Hill area grew. Today, at the southern end, there is no number 1 St. Michael's Place, it seems to have been accommodated into 32 Victoria Road. Similarly at the north end, what would have been number 21 on the north west corner, and number 22 on the north east corner, do not exist, but instead have been numbered as Clifton Hill. While the building of these high density large homes shows the strong demand to live on Church Hill, there was in fact quite a delay before this street was built. Once 1 and 2 Clifton Hill were occupied by 1848, and numbers 3 and 4 were occupied a couple of years later, the owners had a clear view south for nearly twenty years, across Trocke's

Field to the newly built houses at the top of Montpelier Villas. These must have been exciting times for the residents, watching building work commence on their new parish church in 1861, and just across Montpelier Road, on land north of the Temple School, was the market garden of George Parsons – 'Florist and Seedsman to The Queen' (Kelly's Directory 1846). The reason for the five year delay in building St. Michael's Place is not clear. Logically either the developer was short of funds or he used it as a modern day 'land bank', waiting for values to rise, or the sheer scale of the proposed terraces on top of the hill caused the authorities to question it. To the east, Powis Road was started in early 1852, and in Folthorp's Directory of that date there is just one resident, Robert Witney, tea dealer, with no number. This road, having by now assumed its separate identity from Clifton Road, is described as 'Arranged to lead from Clifton Hill, opposite Clifton Road, to the Victoria Road'. By 1854 it still has only four residents: at number 1 is Mrs. Bridget Downs a milliner; number 2 has William and Joseph Sturgess, tailors; number 3 is Henry Prescott a grocer; and at number 5 is William King the dairyman. These details are from the 1854 street directory, and as an illustration of the difficulties with these early publications, the rate book of the same year (ESRO BH/B/4/37/2) lists William and Joseph Sturgess at 1 Powis Road, rather than number 2, and Henry Prescott at 2 rather than number 3. West of St. Michael's Place, a start was made on Denmark Terrace in late 1864, with the first listing in Page's Directory of 1865. Henry Powell, MD lived at number 1, with Robert Bayly, Esq at number 3. The entry then reads, 'And other houses unfinished', describing the Terrace as 'extending from Victoria Road to Clifton Hill'. By 1868, when the first two homes in St. Michael's Place were occupied, fifteen of the twenty-two houses in Denmark Terrace were occupied, with a repeat of the phrase 'And other houses unfinished'.

In Kemp's will the southern boundary to Yearsley's purchase was described as a road leading from Montpelier Road to the Workhouse. It became Victoria Road, but while the south to north connecting roads were being constructed during the 1840s and early 50s – Montpelier Villas, Montpelier Street and Victoria Street leading up from Upper North Street – Victoria Road itself was still unnamed and undeveloped at this stage. As was often the case, its first residential properties were the end-homes of these roads leading up to it. However, there was one exception, noted in chapter 2. The land for the present numbers 14 and 15 Victoria Road was sold by Kemp in 1834, with the two houses built by 1838. So at this time, these two homes, together with Hampton Villa and the Windmill Inn, formed a triangle of large homes with open fields from north to south, with just a few terraced homes being developed between the Villa and the inn. As was seen in chapter 5, the lower slopes of these open fields were known as 'West Hill part of The West Laine', and Kemp was the original landowner. A little further east along Upper North Street, in the 1844 Poor Rate Book (ESRO BH/B/4/35/2) is listed a group of tenements called Chalk Pit Island. They are all owned by E. Butler, numbered 1–7 and described as being between Regent Hill and Regent Row. It seems a reasonable guess that these were named after the chalk pit where Corp. Staines lived at the turn of the century, but for the description of their location to include Regent Hill, it implies they were south of Upper North Street, not on the northern side where the chalk pit itself was. Presumably they were demolished to make way for the terraced homes that completed the last part of Upper North Street as it joined Church Hill opposite Wykeham Terrace. These homes can clearly be seen in the c1850 Newman lithograph illustrated in chapter 2. With Chalk Pit Island being tenements so near to the Workhouse, they may well have been associated with the Mount Sion Place tenements which are also mentioned in chapter 2.

The two previous coloured engravings of the Temple illustrated Church Hill in 1827 and 1835, viewed from the north and east, before a house had been built. The detail of this black and white lithograph above, republished from Yeakell & Gardner's original copper plate 1779 map of Brighton, illustrates Church Hill from the sea, also before a house had been built. This print contains the most complete representation of Church Hill – West Side before any development had taken place. It shows the chalk pit, in shadow, that became the home of Corp. Staines. As the finances of Kemp Town became more difficult because of the economic recession, Kemp started by selling small building plots, hence the triangle of isolated houses mentioned above. Then he, or his widow, sold larger surrounding tracts of land, so the Halletts purchased part of West Hill in 1830; Kemp left for France in 1837; there was the large auction with limited success in 1842; and the widow Kemp sold the area on Church Hill West Side to Yearsley in 1846. Victoria Road first appears in Folthorp's Directory of 1850, and as often happens when a road is first listed, an explanation of its location is given, so it is described as 'at the end of Vine Place – to Montpelier Road'.

By 1850 various traders are occupying numbers 1, 2, 3 and 6 Victoria Road, on the south side, and then terrace homes are added either side of the two houses of 1838, creating the present day terrace on the north side, between Powis Villas and Powis Road. And some interesting residents moved in. Lewis Slight, clerk of the town commissioners, lived in St. Alban's Villa, and his near neighbour was George Faithfull, MP. These first two houses mentioned earlier, built in the late 1830s, were originally listed as Vine Place, there being no other road name to identify them. In 1848 Samuel Weller was living in Selby Villa, Vine Place, with his neighbour Miss Dickson in Linkfield Lodge, Vine Place. By Folthorp's 1850 Directory the new listing for Victoria Road is Samuel Weller, Selby Villa, then George Faithfull, then Miss Harriet Dixon (a different spelling) in Linkfield Lodge. Selby and Linkfield appear to be the early names for 14 and 15 Victoria Road, although which way around is difficult to know: no names are

Detail of 'A Perspective View of Brighthelmston – 1765.'
Lithograph by Day & Son from Henry Martin's *History of Brighton and Environs*, published by John Beal, Brighton 1871. Copied from James Lambert's line engraving of 1765.

This illustration shows the original 'Spring Walk', from the Steine up to St. Nicholas' Church, before Church Street was established a little to the south. The pathway would have been called 'Spring Walk' as it was the pedestrian route up the hill to the chalybeate spring.

visible on the houses today, and there was a change in the numbering during the mid 1850s. Slight's son, Lewis jnr., is also listed with his father, but by 1861 the son is living at 6 Clifton Terrace. Thomas Robson – chemist and post office – was at number 4, which premises is now thought to be the barbers' opposite the church, for reasons explained in chapter 3.

Lewis Slight would have known Henry Faithfull, T.R.Kemp, and his uncle Nathaniel, very well. They were town commissioners, and Slight senior was their clerk. He would also have known John Yearsley and George Cheesman father and son, in their capacity as headboroughs in the town, as well as through their land development and building activities. During this second quarter of the nineteenth century five of the houses in the centre of Montpelier Crescent had rear gardens which reached right up to the western side of Clifton Road, similar to some of the Powis Square gardens reaching to Clifton Hill, as shown in the following map.

The top end of the hill, beside the Children's Hospital, where the road is quite narrow, has no residential buildings, but on the southern side it does have a large flint barn beside what used to be the hospital staff car park. Carder (1990) assumed that this car park was the site of Vine's Mill (although the hospital deeds show that the mill was a few yards to the south west) and he then mentions the barn:

'The adjacent flint building, richly decorated with lions' heads, classical busts and other figurines, may have been connected with this mill, but is generally believed to have been erected in the early nineteenth century as a coach house; it was restored in 1989.'

According to the hospital deeds this barn was built in 1852 as a private coach house when 5 Powis Villas was built. Residential maps of the 1870s show the barn incorporated in the gardens to that house, although the deeds show that the barn was acquired by the hospital in 1870.

Robert Gregory confirms that the first residential building on the Church Hill –West Side was the small house on the corner of Vine Place and Dyke Road, later the miller Vine's home, which was definitely there in 1808. This ties in with Simmons' suggestion of late 1806 for the building of Vine's Mill, and is certain to be the house referred to in the *Sussex Weekly Advertiser*, 20th July 1818, when the mill that became Vine's was offered for auction, together with the mill owner's house, described as 1 Mill Place. The early name for the pathway known as Vine Place was Mill-place. On the 1825 Pigott-Smith map the only houses shown are the mill workers' cottages and this larger mill owner's home on the corner of Vine Place. Gregory also confirms that the origin of Vine Place was as the burial path used to get from Hove church, when it lay in a state of

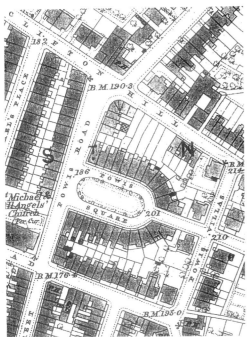

This map from 1875 shows the long gardens of five of the homes on the northern side of Powis Square, reaching up to Clifton Hill. It also illustrates the exclusive nature of the four detached homes that make up the west side of Powis Villas.

disrepair in the eighteenth and early nineteenth centuries, to burials in St. Nicholas' (note 5).

These single storey mill workers' cottages in Vine Place may also have served Clifton Gardens Windmill, which was built c1800 on the land that is now the private gardens of Clifton Terrace. This date of 1808 for the miller's cottage means that his neighbour on Church Hill, just the down the hill past the church, was Corporal Staines, mentioned in the vestry book of 1809 (see chapter 1). The third and final resident on the Hill in the first decade of the nineteenth century was William Shelley, the beadle to St. Nicholas' (see chapter 2).

It is known that Vine's Mill and its accompanying dwelling known as 1 Mill-place was bought by William Vine in August 1818, and after his death in 1836 his wife Mary continued the business until the early 1840s, when Edward Cuttress took it over. The mill was pulled down in about 1849/50, and it seems that when numbers 2 and 3 Powis Villas were built, and possibly Yearsley's own house at number 4, they had the windmill as their neighbour the other side of the road for several months. This demolition of Vine's Mill, and presumably the sale of the land by Cuttress, reminds us that this north-eastern end of Powis Villas was never included in Yearsley's original land purchase and was not developed by him, although it seems likely that the south eastern end of Powis Villas was. This explains why 5 Powis Villas, later called Aberdeen Lodge, with its Italianate tower, oval window and imposing image, is so uncharacteristic of Yearlsey's more restrained style which is evident in Clifton Villa and the detached homes on the west side of Powis Villas. Dawes mentions two fields just below Vine Place which about this time were owned by a butcher named Russell, who let them out to people arranging boxing matches. This would have been the land now occupied by Clifton Terrace and the gardens.

The deeds of number 7 Vine Place refer to an 'ice well', which had been acquired from the rear garden of 10 Powis Grove. It was a circular, unlined chalk-pit about six feet in diameter, and the Sussex Industrial Archaeology Society rediscovered it in 1979, when it was filled in and covered. There were many ice wells in the Centurion and St. Nicholas Road area. The ice, usually imported from the Baltic, was used for making cold confection and chilling wine.

The first homes in Powis Grove were started in 1851, with their first listing appearing in Folthorp's Directory of 1852. 1 Powis Grove was Mrs. Load's boarding school for boys, and number 4 was the home of T.H. Stone Esq. This new road is described as 'Leading from Church Hill, opposite the Workhouse, to Powis Villas'. By 1854 Mrs. Load's school had become Church Hill House, owned by Mrs. Keene, Mr. Stone's number 4 was called Grove Lodge and numbers 2 and 3 were also occupied. Additional unnumbered homes listed were Weston Villa, Powis Cottage and Miss Windle in Derby Villa. Presumably this was one of the Windle family mentioned in chapter 3 as financial sponsors of St. Michael and All Angels'. Of these named houses only Powis Cottage, number 12, is still identifiable today. It is assumed that this house was one of the original Vine Place homes, being the number 5 which is now missing, and had its front entrance changed to be in Powis Grove. By 1859 number 2 Powis Grove had become a ladies school owned by the Misses Booke. Numbers 1 to 7 and 11 and 12 were occupied, but 8, 9 and 10 were vacant.

Mid-nineteenth maps in the Brighton History Centre do clear up one anomaly. The name of 'Clifton', in the Terrace, Hill and Road are all on the west side of Church Hill, but Clifton Street is strangely divorced, on the other side of the hill near the station. The maps explain that they were in fact joined. The continuation of the line of Clifton Road, across Dyke Road, is now called Compton Avenue, but it was originally all Clifton Road, and where it joins Buckingham Place is just a few yards from the northern end of Clifton Street. In the 1856 Directory Clifton Street is described as 'leading from Clifton Road to Buckingham Terrace, at the back of the houses in Terminus Road'. The change of name to Compton Avenue might be explained by an entry in Folthorp's 1856 Directory. As it lists the residents from south to north, it goes up to All Saints Church, then reads 'Compton Terrace, on the opposite side, accounts for the omitted numbers 42 to 57'. Maybe this terrace of later homes on the north-western end of Clifton Road had originally taken its name from Compton Lodge, the large home high on the side of the valley that looked down over Ireland's Pleasure Gardens and Hanover Crescent. This building is now 49 Buckingham Place and called St. Anne's House. There are no definitive notes on the origin of the name Clifton, but it is not unique to Brighton. It may derive from the description of a 'town on a cliff, or hill'. Alternatively the name may have connections with the proximity of a spa or curative mineral spring (the chalybeate – now St. Ann's Well) as it did with the Bristol suburb. A connection with spring water would tie in with the naming of 'Montpelier' Road, as in the French spa name, which is spelt with a double 'll' as was Montpelier Road itself until about 1850.

Steel engraving of Hove Church by J.Tingle after a drawing by G. Atwick. It was published by J. Smith, 8 Pool Valley – undated.

This illustration is a detail from the above steel engraving of Hove Church , with a date of c1845. It shows two windmills on the horizon. The mill on the right is Hodson's, the one left of centre would have been Dyke Road Mill. The houses in front of Hodson's mill are part of the Clifton/Powis/Montpelier estate during its mid-nineteenth development, as viewed from Hove Church, over a mile away. The large house surrounded by trees is Wick House, behind which stood the Temple. This engraving of Hove Church gives us, by chance, a rare view of our area, as seen from the south-west, before the intervening fields were developed.

Gray's notes establish that John Yearsley was the man who named the Powis area, so it is worth looking briefly at his family home, Grove Villa and his foundry business in Brighton. In chapter 7 his wider involvement in the town is explained. From the Brighton History Centre's street directories the following dates emerge. Yearsley was a partner with Robert Williams in an ironmonger's and foundry business. Geoffrey Mead confirms that their foundry, known as Williams and Yearsley's Eagle Foundry, was at the bottom of Gloucester Road, (Gloucester Lane in the 1843 Directory) on the site of the George Beard public house (formerly the Eagle pub), not far from the station. The name of the Eagle Foundry seems to appear before Williams and Yearsley in the Trade Directory of 1826. The partnership also ran an ironmonger's shop at 26 North Street, listed in Leppard's Directory in 1839. While not far from the station, Williams and Yearsley would not have got much business from the new railway as the station workshops had their own foundry works. But there was a great deal of business available, with balconies, balconettes, staircases, bannisters and fireplaces for all the new houses being built throughout the town. Cast iron had become a favoured building material for structural as well as decorative work, so apart from being included in every house that was built at this time, it was widely used in the new station, the West Pier, the Madeira arches and many of the new hotels of the period. The early Victorian iron foundries of Brighton were very busy.

'The Victoria Fountain, Brighton'. Lithograph by W.L. Walton after T. Earp.
Published by W.H. Mason, May 26th 1846, the day the fountain was
officially unveiled.The Royal Albion Hotel is on the left.
To the right is the Royal York Hotel.

The large Victoria Fountain at the southern end of the Steine, designed by A.H. Wilds and erected in 1846 to commemorate the Queen's 27th birthday, was cast by the Eagle Foundry, under Yearsley's ownership (illustrated above). They charged £989 16s 7d to cast the fountain and £114. 7s 6d for setting it in place, most of which was raised by public subscription. The water was supplied from the reservoir of the Brighton Water Works Company, situated on the west side of the Race Hill and conveyed to the fountain by an underground pipe. The water was drawn off through a pipe into Pool Valley, where it was used for supplying the street-cleaning water carts (Fleet 1847). In the Directories of the early 1840s there are eighteen ironmongers listed in Brighton, and with the various foundries in the town, they represented the final chapter in the long history of the British iron industry in the Weald of Surrey, Kent and Sussex. Their heritage stretched from Iron Age Roman Britain, having two of the earliest shaft smelting furnaces near Crawley. By the end of the eighteenth century the local industry was in rapid decline, with just a brief revival in mining near Wadhurst when deposits were found during the building of the railway there in the late 1850s.

In the 1846 Kelly's Directory there are no Powis addresses listed (which is in line with Gray's notes). Numbers 1 to 8 are listed in Clifton Road, and as mentioned, Clifton Hill just has Charles Curtis at the Crescent Inn, James Killner the wheelwright in Clifton Mews and James Tyler, a bookseller living in Clifton Cottage. Gray's notes say that Yearsley commenced his development in 1847, the first house completed being Powis House, Powis Place. As noted earlier, Powis Place was the neck that joined the Square to Powis Villas, and is now part of Powis Square. In Rapkin's Map of Brighton in 1852, the whole of Powis Square is called Powis Place. This stage of the development is confirmed in Folthorp's 1848 Directory, which contains the first mention of Powis. The entry reads:

Powis Place: Upper part of Vine-pl. Church Hill.
Sharpe, Mr. Edward.
Sharpe, Mr. David, Powis House.

Although this is 1848, and the deeds to 3 Powis Villas mention April 1849 as the date for the sale of the land of 3 Powis Villas to Mr. Sharpe, presumably this entry in Folthorp's of Powis Place, Upper part of Vine Place, does in fact refer to the house now known as 3 Powis Villas. It is on the corner site of the Villas and that part of Powis Square which was first called Upper Powis Place. Sharpe purchased the land from John Yearsley once the house had been built, and the possibility is that Sharpe had the house built on Yearley's leasehold land, sometime during 1847 or '48, and then bought the freehold land as soon as

Yearsley was able to sell it. This explains the slight difference in date between the directory entry and the land sale in the deeds. Also in this 1848 Directory, Yearsley is confirmed as living in Clifton Villa, Clifton Hill. There are two more reasons for believing that this 1848 entry reading Powis Place actually refers to Powis Villas.

First, the next Folthorp Directory of 1850 reads:

Powis Villas:
2 Sharp. Mr. Edward.
(The name Sharp appears variously with or without the final 'e')
3 Sharp. Mr. David.
4 Yearsley. Mr. John, Grove villa.

This rather implies that Powis Villas was not so named until late 1849, a few months after Yearsley finally purchased the freehold. The second reason is seen on the following map. Numbers 2 and 3 Powis Villas were detached homes, but the following 1853 map shows the two houses as attached to the terrace in the neck of Powis Place, which simply continues the early description of their address from the 1848 directory. The other interesting aspect of this evolution of addresses is that 3 Powis Villas was originally called Powis House, and on the west side number 4 was the third house to be built, while number 1 was in fact the fourth and final Powis Villa to be built on this side.

Above is number 2 Powis Villas, first owned by Edward Sharp in 1848 and described as being 'Powis Place – Upper part of Vine Place'. The name 'Vine Place' originally carried on through what is now Victoria Road, and until Powis Villas was so named the name of 'Vine' obviously extended up the hill, despite the fact that Clifton Hill had been named by this date.

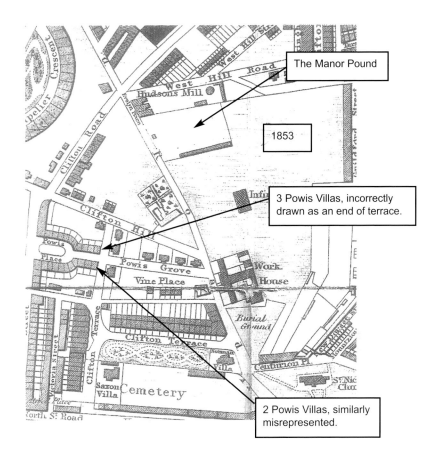

The Manor Pound

1853

3 Powis Villas, incorrectly drawn as an end of terrace.

2 Powis Villas, similarly misrepresented.

This 1853 map also illustrates the extensive grounds belonging to the Workhouse, and shows the 'Manor Pound' which Erredge writes about as being moved up to the north-west corner of the Workhouse estate in 1824. It also shows the top part of Church Street, where it joins Dyke Road, named as Centurion Place, and the building on the northern side of Centurion Place is Bennett's the Stonemason with Shelley's tenements.

Gray's notes continue:

'In 1849 a start was made on Powis Villas. Mr. Yearsley had a house built for his own occupation, Grove Villa, the present number 4 Powis Villas, and lived there until his death in 1857.'

This house was subsequently owned by Dr. John Coombes, who purchased it in 1993. He re-named it Grove House, taking the name of the house where Dr. Coombes himself was born.

Gray's notes again:

'Nos. 2 & 3 (Powis Villas) were built in 1849. By 1852 nos.1 to 8 inclusive had been completed. The four houses, 10, 11, 12 and 13 Powis Villas, the short terrace on the south-eastern side, were the last to be built, being erected by 1853 and all occupied by June 1854.'

As noted, this first date of 1849 quoted by Gray is not quite in line with Folthorpe's note of the two Sharpes living there in 1848. However, 1849 is the date of Yearsley's freehold purchase, which may have signalled the speeding-up of the development, and seems to be the year that Powis Villas was named, so it could easily have been a date that Gray particularly remembered. The rest of Gray's dates are born out by Taylor's Directory of 1854 – Powis Grove has eight residents, Powis Square has seventeen residents listed, and the Villas have twelve residents, with John Yearsley living at number 4, Grove Villa. In this same Directory Clifton Hill is listed with fourteen residents, but no numbers to the houses, although numbers had been assumed and later changed, according to the April 1847 deeds previously mentioned. In the directories John Taylor is in the livery stables, Clifton Mews, but in the 1851 census he describes himself as 'Fly Proprietor', (an entry in the 1848 Brighton Directory reads 'hackney coaches are here (B/ton) called flys'). Taylor was living with his wife Mary, a servant and a driver. By this date the house known as Lone Cottage had become separated from the business of the Mews. While Taylor's postal address is 12 (that is, the house in the Mews), Lone Cottage itself, number 13, is described as a lodging-house, occupied by John Hawkins, a labourer, and his wife Mary, a laundress. The census also indicates there were two daughters, four sons and four building labourers lodging in the house as well. This number of residents suggests that the extension to the back of Lone Cottage, since it was run as a laundry by Mrs. Watts in 1839, had taken place by 1847 at the latest.

Looking at Powis Square and Montpelier Crescent it is easy to miss the fact that this is the only conservation area in the centre of town that can boast its own Square and its own Crescent. Squares and Crescents were made a feature of seafront architecture, with the obvious effect of giving the maximum number of households a sea view. Once all the available seafront sites had been built on, this residential format moved inland, no doubt taking the lead from the influence of the late eighteenth century London squares. In the town, Russell, Clarence and Norfolk Squares had glimpses of a sea view when first built, but the other inland crescents, Hanover and Park, were well away from the seafront. Interestingly, Montpelier Crescent and the much smaller Hanover Crescent were both built to the same orientation, each looking west-north-west.

When Powis Square and Montpelier Crescent were first built, also facing in a similar direction, both offered their residents beautiful views westward, over the countryside to Blatchington, to the restored church of St. Andrews, Hove, and, for some of the homes, a distant view of the Channel off the natural harbour at Shoreham. Musgrave (1981) describes the houses of Montpelier Crescent as being on 'the grandest scale in all of A.H. Wilds' work'. Professor Robson gives them further architectural importance, describing the Crescent, out of all Brighton's residential developments, as the point at which Regency architecture ended and Victorian architecture began. Robson & Macdonald (1987) describe A.H. Wilds as producing 'powerful and attractive Regency buildings well into the Victorian period' and that the Wilds father and son, with Busby, 'played a significant part in the final stages of the last great period of architectural consensus in this country'.

Montpelier Crescent is the third of Amon Henry Wilds' four great crescents, three in Brighton and one in Worthing, and undoubtedly has a very important place in the architectural history of our city. Its orientation is interesting. At the time of building there was sufficient land to have the main body of the Crescent at a right angle to Montpelier Road, facing due south, with every home bathed in sunshine much of the summer, all enjoying sea views, and with Clifton Hill as the boundary road to the private parkland in the front. As it is, the homes at the northern end are the main recipients of sunshine into their front rooms, and this in the afternoon as the sun is setting. Was Wilds thinking of the ruinous effect of bright sunlight on soft furnishings and the hand-coloured engravings that would have graced most of the sitting rooms and bedrooms at the front of these homes? Or had this west-north-west orientation met with sufficient approval in the smaller Hanover Crescent that it was worth repeating? When it was initially built it must have created an impressive sight for the many travellers approaching Brighton from the west, particularly those on the railway line from Shoreham, before the train disappeared into the cutting that took the passengers around the north side of Church Hill and into the station. The Crescent was built on the lower western slopes of Church Hill, with the chalybeate spring, Wick and Hove Village all looking up to it, until Vernon Terrace was built some ten years later.

As the western limit of Brighton, with green fields in front, it was a very imposing sight. It consists of thirty-eight homes, taking in the end houses that are actually on Montpelier Road, and building square rooms on the acute part of a curve presents its own set of problems. But Wilds managed to keep all the rooms square by incorporating the difficult angles into the entrance-hall links between the large Palladian facades. And it was these imposing facades that appealed to the particular rising middle-class market, many from London, who wanted to live in large villas but could not afford the detached version. The fashionable solution to this market's needs, established in London, was to build these imposing facades with such a unity that each one looked like a large single mansion. Behind this illusory façade there were two, and sometimes three, homes with many of the front entrances set sufficiently well back at the sides to confirm the impression of detached villas, as clearly shown in the next illustration (page 98).

In Brighton, Montpelier Crescent is the best example of this architectural sleight of hand. The homes are not actually detached, but they do not look like a terrace either, and they appear to be much larger than they really are. In effect they are a clever nineteenth-century example of a phrase that developers use today – each villa façade hiding its pair or three homes, is 'link-detached', linked by the entrance hall. Dale (1947) suggests the south and north ends, numbers 1 to 6 and 34 to 38, were added later, rather than built while the main crescent was under construction. However, various clues tell us that these end homes were in the original plan. They were simply built last and for a different clientele – one that didn't aspire to live in what looked like a large detached town villa. First, the engraving of the Crescent illustrated in chapter 8 clearly shows the most southerly houses had not been built, but Kelly's 1846 Directory lists a Mrs. Maillard living at number 2. This bears out the author's suggested date of c1845 for this print. Also a map of 1847 shows the houses reaching down to the Clifton Hill junction, and up to the Dyke Road turning. As the development unfolded, the first built middle section of villas, numbers 7 to 31, all had the central pediment on the front elevation, but this design was abandoned at either end. And Wilds carefully planned the allocation of whether each complete frontage contained two or three homes in it. The pairs are all in the central section from 16 to 25, while the sets of three houses are contained in each of the last three villas at either end. So the largest homes were in the centre of the crescent shape. As the houses moved out from the centre they became smaller, but still part of what looked like a detached residence, then at the end wings you bought a large terraced house that did not pretend to be anything else. As usual the fronts were built, and the house of the individual's choice and purse was then added behind.

The practical problem of access to the backs of the facades, for the enormous task of building two or three houses behind each one, was solved by using routes or trackways that were abutting the Crescent grounds but were at this stage undeveloped themselves. These were the lower part of Clifton Hill (still called the Blatchington Road as the building work began), the land at the rear, that became the western side of Clifton Road, and the last few yards of Dyke Road before it met Montpelier Road. On early maps of the Crescent all the central gardens reach up to the boundary of what became Clifton Road, but it seems reasonable to assume that these last few yards of gardens were always intended for the development of the west side of Clifton Road. In Hanover Crescent the cobbled wall still establishes the front edge of the estate, and in the following engraving it looks as if Montpelier Crescent was given a similar edging, but no trace of such a wall stands today. In chapter 7 the March 1845 deed details the development of the 'new road', as Clifton Road was then called, although this road features on a map of 1842, but with no buildings at that stage. This 1842 date showing it as a route rather than a residential road is in line with Clifton Road's origins as the link between Western Road at Hampton Place and the newly built railway station. These dates are also confirmed by the various Town Rate Books in the ESRO, where the name Clifton does not appear in the books of 1840, 1844 or 1845, which is in line with the naming of Clifton Hill.

Regarding the illusion of large crescent villas, where in fact they are two or three separate homes, this technique was also successfully used in the ten pairs of semi-detached houses of Montpelier Villas, where individual entrances are also tucked at either side of what looks like one large home. To enhance this 'single villa illusion' in Montpelier Villas, Wilds kept each pair of semi-detached homes on the same horizontal plane, rather than stepping each home down the slope of the road. It is not clear when the jump was made from the not uncommon semi-detached estate workers' cottages of the Georgian period to the new middle class semi-detached town villas, but it is possible that Montpelier Villas was at the forefront of this architectural innovation being used in an entire street. Certainly there is no other early Victorian residential road like it in Brighton. Couple this fact to the unique example of the small detached villas that make up the west side of Powis Villas (see chapter 9), the other semi-detached homes in that road and the two pairs at the bottom of Clifton Hill, together with the 'link-detached' mansions in Montpelier Crescent – all having been built between 1843 and 1850 – and it becomes clear that this conservation area is a remarkable and unique example of the emerging architectural style of the early Victorian middle classes. It is also interesting to remember that these new homes of the richer middle class merchants and business owners, some built with their illusion of size, were side by side to the new homes of the Brighton builders, carpenters and craftsmen who, while building larger houses for their richer clients, were creating classic terrace homes for themselves, with no attempts at 'illusions of grandeur'. Even the Clifton Terrace homes, of which the local builder Richard Edwards owned a few, with the late Regency-style charm and cohesion that is so appreciated today, did not pretend to be anything other than terraced houses.

Of course the middle classes had been catered for to some degree in the 1820s and 30s, with the Brunswick development and the intentions behind Kemp Town. But in those plans their houses were just an added element to the imposing squares for the gentry, and they were carefully put in their place behind the grand facades. In the Clifton, Montpelier and Powis area things were very different - the tradesmen, dealers and business people were in charge.

From this detail of the Montpelier Crescent engraving (illustrated in full in chapter 8), it can be seen how the artist clearly shows that the recessed front entrances give the intended illusion of large detached villas. Like the St. Michael and All Angels' print in chapter 3, this is another example of a London engraver getting the position of sunlight and shadows in Brighton completely the wrong way around, with the sun apparently shining from due north. However one detail the artist has portrayed faithfully is the division of the villas into pairs and threes. The sets of three houses at either end have uninterrupted rows of windows from one side to the other. The larger pairs in the central section have the column of decorative window shapes under the central pediment, with two windows either side. These are not windows that have been filled in because of the tax, they are Wilds' formula for dividing the villas into two homes, with an equal number of windows to each. Regarding the window tax, in 1844 Brighton paid to the national revenue £15,912 (Fleet 1847) and Kelly's 1846 Directory, in a section on the town's wealth, reports that 'in its contribution to the Window-Tax the town ranks third in the kingdom'.

As the area developed towards the mid 1850s, slight class distinctions were already creeping into the various roads. Clifton Terrace in 1856 had no tradespeople on its main frontage, just Mr. Travis in the Clifton Arms Inn around the corner looking down Victoria Road, and a tea-dealer and grocer opposite. Clifton Road, Powis Villas and Square similarly advertised no shops or trades

– their absence ensured by early building covenants.

Clifton Hill on the other hand could be viewed as not quite so exclusively residential. It included the livery stables in Clifton Mews, a bootmaker, two laundresses, a green-grocer, a bookseller and wool shop, Fred Wright's chemist and tobacconist and the Crescent Inn. By the early 1860s Victoria Road had James Field the grocer, Thomas Robson the chemist and Post Office Receiving House, William Powell the stationer, Thomas Lanaway the butcher and Christopher Sharp, a baker. Similarly, down the hill towards Western Road, the residents of Hampton Place were supported by the trades in Hampton Street, where in 1845 numbers 2 & 3 were livery stables, and number 4 was a builder. And in the 1846 directory Sillwood Place was gentry while Sillwood Street (first called Bedford Square Road in the 1841 census) was home to the supporting traders.

The only other nineteenth century steel engraving of Montpelier Crescent is by J.S. & Co. taken from the northern end, illustrated below. On the right-hand margin can be seen the end of Vernon Terrace, the development of which was started 1855/56. This illustration also shows the illusion of detached villas that Wilds had so successfully created. From this print it looks as if the northern entrance to the Crescent was enclosed with gardens and railings. The final part of this northern end of the Crescent, directly facing us in the picture, no longer exists. It was knocked down to provide space for the Seven Dials junction, with a fairly sympathetic side wall built, as the next photograph shows.

99

This view is from the same position as the J.S. & Co. print of the Crescent,
both showing the junction of Montpelier Crescent with the Road from Henfield, c1857,
and the Seven Dials junction in 2007.
The trees in the Crescent area now obscure the view of the houses
that could be seen in the mid-nineteenth engraving.

The detail of the left-hand side of the first Montpelier Crescent engraving, on the following page, dated as has been suggested c1845, shows houses behind the northern end of the crescent. These would be the buildings on Dyke Road just as it arrives at the junction that was to become the Seven Dials. From the configuration of the windows, it looks as if these are the fronts of the houses on the northern side of Dyke Road, rather than the backs of any houses on the southern side. There is no other nineteenth century engraved image of these Dyke Road buildings, and they were demolished with the development of the junction.

The houses on the far left were on the northern side of
Dyke Road as it arrived at the junction with
Montpelier Road and the Crescent. From the window
shapes it looks as if they were private homes
rather than shops. As the northern end of the curve of the
Crescent was demolished for the building
of the Seven Dials junction, so were these early
homes on Dyke Road.

7

John Yearsley's Brighton Interests

John Yearsley's signature – 30th October 1849

The first mention of John Yearsley is in the 1833 Brighton Directory, where under the Municipal Guide, coming after magistrates and clerk to the High Constable, he is one of eight men listed as headboroughs. This was an office established in the time of King Alfred, with the title continuing through the eighteenth century honorary officials, elected annually, 'to act occasionally for the preservation of the peace, in keeping public houses in order, and on special occasions', (Kelly's 1846). Bearing in mind our particular interest in Mr. Yearsley is centered around the late 1840s, this earlier position of responsibility indicates he was an established figure in the town.

By the late 1840s Yearsley was involved with a number of properties in our area. Joy Moore (c1970), in her essay on this area, mentions Yearsley's partnership in the Eagle Foundry, the building by him of 5 Clifton Hill and of Clifton Villa in which he lived, and of Grove Villa, his final home. Joy Moore lived at 28 Montpelier Street, and found further investments in the area by Yearsley mentioned in her deeds, she writes:

'In 1849 the owner of my house, John Yearsley, paid off the mortgage which Stephen Davey held. The next door house, No. 27, was also listed in the 1848 ratebook as belonging to Yearsley, not Stephen Davey as in 1846; perhaps a similar transaction took place.'

1849 was a busy year for Yearsley. He was selling Clifton Villa and moving into the new and much larger Grove Villa, probably in the latter part of the year, and paying off mortgages on other properties. The name of Davey, this time Edward, appears again with Yearsley in the list of headboroughs. In 1851 John

Yearsley is also recorded as owning a small plot of land, three rods, up near Queens Park, between what is now Richmond Street and Sussex Street. He paid a 7s 6d rate to the vicar. Also by 1851 he is a trustee of the Brighton & Hove Benefit Building Society. Yearsley's involvement in Montpelier Street is enlarged upon in a deed of covenant dated 20th March 1845, which is in the possession of a previous owner of 2 Powis Villas. It is a deed in respect of property on Terminus Road, Brighton, between John Yearsley, with Messrs. Juniper and Wood ironmongers, Mr. Richard Chapman, who was a town commissioner, Mr. John Smith and Mr. William Watts, and concerns their agreement on the development of several pieces of ground 'situated on the south eastern side of and adjoining the new road leading from Hampton Place in Brighton to the London and Brighton Railway Station'. On today's map this 'new road', going from south to north, is made up of Hampton Place, Montpelier Street, Powis Road, Clifton Road, Compton Avenue and part of Buckingham Place extending into Terminus Road. The 'new road from Hampton Street to the Railway Terminus' is also mentioned in the July 1859 deeds of 16 Clifton Hill.

The earlier mentioned deed of March 1845 tells us that Yearsley, with partners as usual, owned and developed various parcels of land along this 'new road', which ran along the western boundary of the near three acres he purchased from Kemp a year later. Montpelier Street is part of this new road, but from the deed's descriptions it is clear that it relates to the development of that part of the 'new road' which is today called Clifton Road. The deed stipulates that there will be a dwarf boundary wall with iron railings to a height of 5' 6" and that no building will be erected nearer than 14' 6" to this wall. It also informs us that Yearsley owned the first 76' of frontage on the road, William Watts, laundryman, (mentioned in chapter 4) owned the next 76', then Juniper and Wood (ironmongers) 50', Watts the next 50', Watts and Chapman 25', Watts and Smith 25' and finally Watts owned the last 50'. These details from the privately held 1845 deeds are repeated in the ESRO document AMS 6345 and the plots of 25' width were for one house. The corner site, where Clifton Road joins the Hill, is Clifton Villa, where Yearsley lived before his Powis Villas home was built, and the houses on the east side of Clifton Road, running northwest from Clifton Villa, all have the aforementioned dwarf wall with iron railings up to 5' 6", and a front garden about 15' deep. Along the passage of the 'new road' from Hampton Place to the station these houses are the only examples where these two features co-exist. Furthermore, the first four houses are identical, forming the first part of the terrace and covering just under 80' – corresponding to John Yearsley's 76' of frontage. The next four houses, different from the first but again forming a unit, have approximately the same frontage – which belonged to William Watts. Thereafter the units in which matching houses are added to the terrace are smaller, all of which is in line with the ground ownership as described in the deeds.

A letter dated June 1995 from John Tyson, a resident in Clifton Road at the time, confirms that this deed was talking about these houses on Clifton Road. In Mr. Tyson's deeds, in the charges of register, the March 1845 deed between Yearsley, Juniper and Wood etc., is referred to as relating to 3 Clifton Road. This does not reveal whether Yearsley developed the houses that he owned in Montpelier Street, although it seems reasonable to think that he did, but it does confirm his involvement in the development of other properties along this new road, namely Warwick Villa and Down Villa already mentioned in chapter 6. He had the corner house, Clifton Villa – 7 Clifton Hill, built during the summer of 1845, just before he purchased the leasehold on the land for the Powis development. All this changes a previously published suggestion of c1830 for this side of Clifton Road – the land was not purchased for development until 1845. The first four houses on the eastern side of Clifton Road are Grade 2 listed buildings. No. 5, which is in the second terrace of four, was until recently the vicarage of St. Nicholas' Church: apparently it was a gift to the church. Before this, St. Nicholas' Vicarage was at 6 Montpelier Villas, and prior to that it was at 2 Buckingham Road, probably the closest it has ever been to the church itself. On the western side of this part of Clifton Road there are two detached villas either side of two post-war semi-detached houses, which replaced a third detached villa. The deeds to one of these villas, number 26, were kept in London during the war and were lost to enemy action.

Thankfully the owners of number 28 have a copy of the land registry records showing an indenture dated 15th May 1846 between Catherine Hunt and Thomas Wisden, a builder who was later involved in numbers 1 – 4 Clifton Hill. It was noted earlier that Carder (1990) suggests about 1830 for the three-storey homes on the east side of Clifton Road, but this is now known to be some fifteen years too early, and in the same entry he suggests that number 26 was built in the 1820s and 'probably designed by Wilds and Busby'. However, the origins of Clifton Road are tied up with the building of the railway terminus. There was no reason for it to exist as a route before 1841, and the engraving of 'The Temple Grammar School' in chapter 7 illustrates the undeveloped open downland, on which Clifton Road was later built, as it was in 1835. On the maps throughout the 1820s and 1830s the only routes going through our area were from east to west – there were none north to south apart from the boundaries of Montpelier and Dyke Roads. Regarding Carder's thoughts on the designers of the house, Charles Busby (1788–1834) and Wilds senior (1762–1833), both had died several years before the route that became Clifton Road existed. That leaves A.H. Wilds (1784 – 1857), but a past professor of architecture at the old Brighton Polytechnic's School of Architecture attributes the house to a later copyist of the Busby and Wilds' tradition. Thomas Wisden is the obvious name for this house and number 28, but whoever the builder was, they may well have been looking at Busby's first published collection of house designs and modelled the house on the design for 87 London Road. This is a delightful small villa, illustrated as plate 17 in Dale's 'Fashionable Brighton'. The two houses have clear similarities, but the Clifton Road house, with its façade built to the very unusual format of a square, lacks something of the symmetry and balance of the original Busby design. Thomas Wisden is the likely builder as, in the 1840s, he was busy on the large plot of land that formed the western corner of Clifton Hill and Road. In Kelly's 1867 Directory the builder Wisden and Charles Scrase Dickens are listed as 'Lords of The Manor' with George Faithfull and Somers Clarke respectively noted as their stewards. Faithfull and his son were solicitors of 15 Ship Street, and Somers Clarke was a partner in the firm of Attree, Clarke and Howlett, solicitors, of 8 Ship Street. Wisden purchased his share of the Lordship of the Manor of Brighton and Lewes from C.J.V. Hervey for £2,250 on 11th February 1853 (ESRO AMS6167/1/5).

Travelling down to the southern most end of this 'new road' mentioned earlier, there is the site of the old Post Office (there until 2005) on the corner of Hampton Place and Western Road. The Post Office, formerly a bank, has an ornately decorated frontage, which was a later addition built in the front garden of the house called Sutton Lodge, and immediately behind that is Codrington House, the home of Sir Edward Codrington (1770–1851). To the west of Codrington House was an earlier bungalow called Hampton Lodge. For the early part of its life this was the Brighton home of Henry Fauntleroy (1785–1824) the banker of Marsh, Sibbald, Graham, Stracey & Fauntleroy, of Berners Street, London. In September 1824, before much of our area was developed, Fauntleroy was arrested on a charge of forgery. He had been forging signatures to cash in government stock lodged by customers with the bank. He was a well known figure in Brighton, having a number of finely furnished houses, driving splendid carriages and keeping expensive mistresses, but his bank's losses were over £400,000 and they quickly went bankrupt. He was hanged outside Newgate Prison in November 1824, watched by a crowd said to be over 10,000 (Ford 1981), but numbered as 100,000 by Douglas d'Enno (2007). This latter number would have been quite a crowd for 1824. His executioner, the official hangman for Newgate, was James Botting who lived just near West Street, not far from Hampton Lodge itself. Tradition has it that Botting gave his victims a drop of no more than two feet, so their deaths were very slow. (My Brighton & Hove internet site – 2007).

Hampton Lodge was then purchased by Sir Edward Codrington. Codrington was the captain of the *Orion* (74 guns), and was involved in the blockade of Cadiz and the battle of Trafalgar in October 1805. According to the Pigott-Smith map published in 1826, the gardens to Hampton Lodge extended eastwards up to the turning that was to become Hampton Place, and it was on this land that Codrington later developed Codrington House and Sutton Lodge. He is recorded as living in Hampton Lodge in 1832, but by August that year he had let the bungalow to Sir Samuel Shepherd. In the mid 1840s he developed the nine houses in Codrington Place, and either owned numbers 1 and 2 Western Cottages, which later became 1 and 2 Sillwood Road, or owned the land, on which he built two houses. The NatWest bank building now stands on this site, with the result that Sillwood Road starts with number 3.

Codrington Place ran along the southern edge of what is now the Waitrose car park, and was accessed by a road from Western Road, running north alongside the eastern edge of where Waitrose supermarket now stands. The terrace of houses, 1 to 9 Codrington Place, was being built during 1845, with just five of the nine homes appearing in Kelly's 1846 Directory, and numbers 1 to 7 occupied by 1848. They all had large front gardens that formed the northern side of Western Road, as did Hampton Lodge. A later leaseholder of Hampton Lodge, in the mid 1840s, was General Sir Ralph Darling. In May 1899 Sir Edward's grandson, Lt. Col. Alfred Edward Codrington of HM Coldstream Guards, sold this whole estate to William Richard Sutton, of 22 Golden Lane, Middx., for £42,000.

In preparation for this sale, Engall & Co., executors for the late Sir Edward, prepared a report for the estate's sale prospects. It was dated 9th September 1884 and valued Codrington House and Sutton Lodge at £1,850 each and the

'Hampton Lodge,
Fauntleroy's Villa, Brighton.'
Steel engraving – no artist or publisher named.

two houses in Sillwood Road at £1,080 each. Hampton Lodge was let at a yearly rental of £153. 3. 6d and the nine Codrington Place houses were all let at £70 to £80 pa. Engalls reported that 'all the tenants are highly respectable and most satisfactory' (ESRO – AMS 654-659). In Engell's report, the fact that the first four houses mentioned were valued for sale purposes indicates that they were homes for members of Codrington's family, while Hampton Lodge and the Codrington Place houses were let and so had a rental value placed on them. The purchaser of the estate, Sutton, obviously kept it for rental income, and the only house he demolished on the north side of Western Road appears to be Hampton Lodge. Maybe an extravagantly decorated bungalow was not the easiest property to let, and it seems likely that William Sutton was the owner who built the two large houses that replaced the Lodge.

Returning to Grove Villa, John Yearsley died in 1857 and his widow Julia continued to live in the family home, which was held in trust by his brother William. John had come close to death some nine years earlier, with an illness that was reported in the *Brighton Gazette*, and a copy of this local article was published in the *Times* of October 21st 1848. While acting as the foreman of a jury at the Lewes Sessions he was suddenly seized with 'a fit of apoplexy'. The surgeon who attended him fully expected that he would not make it through the night, but in the morning he was able to ask questions 'indicating that he had no recollection whatever of what had passed subsequent to the attack'. In John Yearsley's will (NA PROB 11/2258) the wider family is mentioned. He had an aunt, Anne Weaver, a sister, Sarah Yearsley, and a niece, presumably William's daughter, Mary Yearsley. All his real estate and personal estate was left to his brother William in trust to invest in 'public funds and government securities, his wife to enjoy the same for life and after her death for any children by her to be divided equally . . . ' Maybe his wife was sufficiently younger for him to imagine her marrying again as a widow. He also gave £1,000 to his brother 'as a mark of my affectionate regard for him'. The will was dated 5th January 1854 and valued his personal estate at £6,000. William Yearsley died just three years after his brother, on 19th August 1860.

From the time the houses in Clifton Hill are numbered, the street directories begin to list Grove Villa with two addresses. Folthorp's 1861 and 1862 Directories list Mrs. Yearsley at 4 Powis Villas and then again at 23 Clifton Hill, Grove Villa, in the Court section. At this time Folthorp's became Page's Court Guide and General Directory, and in the intermittent directories up to 1876, Julia Yearsley continues to have this duplicate listing. Also during these dates, in the separate lists of houses and villas in Brighton, the entries for Grove Villa are similarly duplicated. The deeds available for Grove Villa tell us more about the Yearsley family. These deeds only date back to 1876, but they confirm that William Yearsley was John's brother and that John had two daughters, the eldest called Jane, and her sister Julia named after her mother. The youngest daughter Julia married Richard John Cheesman Taaffe, son of Richard P.B. Taaffe, who is listed under medical practitioners as living at 45 Old Steine.

Ken Fines (2004) makes the point that by 1845 Brighton had lost its royal patronage, which was soon replaced by 'rail patronage', and this promoted the second phase of the town's growth. Hitherto there had been a gulf in the social scale between the nobility and gentry of fashionable Brighton and those in trade, commerce and service. The railway led to a much broader social mix, bringing in those who made their money in industry and commerce, together with the professional classes and retired army 'top brass' who were now able to retire to Brighton, or some who had businesses in London. Fines writes, 'It was this class which by and large was to colonize the parish of Hove and the adjoining heights of Montpelier and Clifton Hill.' John Yearsley certainly fits the description and was the right man on Church Hill to take part in this explosion of building work in the town.

While Yearsley was developing Powis, the development of Queens Road was well under way, with £2,000 towards the construction costs provided by the railway company. Raymond Flower (1986) writes, 'The age of the commuter had dawned — rich merchants and stockbrokers found they could travel up to

'Railway Terminus, Brighton.' Wood engraving from *The Land We Live In* – 1854.
While the development of Clifton and Powis was underway, a few hundred yards over the hill the station forecourt was created, together with the cutting down to Trafalgar Street and the access bridge across from Queens Road. In the 1843 Directory the station is described as 'One of the finest structures of the kind in England', and in the ESRO 'New Street plans' DB/D6/14 the application to build the north end of Queens Road and the Trafalgar Street Bridge was submitted on 20th May 1849, the year Powis Villas was being developed

London in the morning for business and return in time for dinner.' Edmund Gilbert (1954) writes that 'By 1853 there was a total of twelve trains daily from Brighton to London, including the 8.45am city express, which did the journey non-stop in eighty minutes.' Travelling up to town and back in a day was not unheard of in the coaching days of course, but it was a twelve-hour round trip, assuming nothing went wrong along the way.

By 1845 there were virtually no coaches left travelling from London. John Farrant in his Erredge reprint notes, 'Not only were Brighton's roles as a resort town diversifying, its economic base was widening, driven above all by the railways. The main line from London had opened in 1841. North of the station the London, Brighton and South Coast Railway Co. located its principal workshops, and from 1852 locomotives were being built there. It employed about 600 men in 1851.' Kelly's Directory for 1867 shows that by this date Brighton Station had over 1,200 engineers involved in building and repairing locomotives, with 150 men employed in the traffic department.

Edmund Gilbert writes that these railway works were also used for marine engineering, and the workshops for steamers were only moved to Newhaven in 1880. In the late 1840s, appreciative of the profits they were making from the increased passenger revenues on race days, the railway companies quadrupled their annual contribution to prize money for Brighton Race Course. Putting the railways' influence in context, during the year of 1837 the mail and stage coaches brought 50,000 passengers to the town. By 1850, at the height of the summer season the railways brought 75,000 visitors in a single week, Underwood (1978). It was precisely this period of astonishing increase in visitor numbers that saw the Church Hill – West Side sheep down turn into Brighton's most important early Victorian residential area.

At this point, another piece of good timing occurred for Yearsley's development. A month after he purchased the leasehold of his land from Kemp's widow, in the September of 1846, the Brighton & Hove General Gas Company entered into an agreement with the town commissioners to provide oil and gas for lighting the Western district of the town, having a contract already in place to supply the Eastern part of Brighton (ESRO AMS6345).

The earlier 'Gas Light and Coke Company' had been established by Act of Parliament in 1818 and there had been examples of gas lighting in Brighton since about 1819, it being installed in the Theatre Royal in July of that year. Its first use in London had been in 1811, lighting Ackermann's Repository of Arts in The Strand. In Baxter's 1822 *Stranger in Brighton* Directory the Gas Light Company claimed to have laid two miles of conducting pipes in all the principal streets and added that 'its introduction into private houses is daily becoming more general'. To put that claim in context, there were only about 150 named streets in the whole of Brighton at that time, not many could be deemed as 'principal', and the majority working population would certainly not have afforded gas-lit homes, although they saw it in the lamps around the Steine by 1824. The Pavilion was among the first buildings to have gaslights, although William IV had them all removed on safety grounds. On the October 1846 agreement document (ESRO DB/B66/58), the Western area is highlighted on a map. Its eastern boundary is the Steine and London Road, south is the seafront, Preston Parish is the northern boundary, and Hove Parish, in a north to south line just west of Montpelier Road, forms the western edge. Montpelier, Clifton and Powis are at the exact centre of this 'Western area'. The wording of the agreement echoed that of the 1839 Act of Parliament, to supply 'any streets, squares, lanes, roads, passages, churches and chapels, theatres, shops and inns and dwelling houses with coal gas, commonly called Carburetted Hydrogen Gas'.

The cost to the new dwelling houses on Church Hill was 7 shillings per one thousand cubic feet of gas supplied by meter consumption. As Yearsley developed the houses, no doubt he also had an eye on the business prospect of supplying the gas company with all the batswings burners, columns, brackets, lamp irons and lamp posts, as well as the range of small and main cast iron pipes and the wealth of iron-ware infrastructure that was necessary. Still in 1846, during the first half of the year the clerk of the town commissioners, Lewis Slight, started negotiations with the gas company regarding the lighting and putting out of all the street lamps at sunrise and sunset. There were 772 public lamps at this time (Fleet 1847) and this work was always carried out by employees of that company, but Slight, with an eye to saving the town money, suggested it should be done by 'servants of the town commissioners'. In a letter dated Feb 9th 1846 (ESRO – above ref.) J. Butler from the gas company offices at Black Rock writes that such an idea is 'without precedent or parallel in the Kingdom', and hopes that Mr. Slight will withdraw that particular condition – but he didn't.

This expansion of supply by the gas company meant that, unlike the gentry's houses in the eastern district of town which had to be converted to gas lighting, much of the Church Hill residential development could be promoted as modern housing with the facilities of the best houses in town – gas lighting was already installed. The gas company was located at Black Rock to avoid the 6d a ton tax on coal landed at Brighton, which was levied all along the Brighton shoreline. Going eastwards, it wasn't until the ships got as far as Black Rock that they escaped Brighton's jurisdiction. The Hove gasworks to the west was there for the same reason. The coal tax came into being with the 1773 Brighton Town Act, and was particularly for the building and upkeep of the groynes.

Having built his first home, Clifton Villa, on land on the northern side of Clifton Hill that Kemp had originally mortgaged to Thomas Budgen, John Yearsley's land purchase from the widow Kemp (leasehold in 1846 and converted to freehold in 1849), was the final area at the top of Church Hill West Side to be developed. Throughout the late 1830s and mid 1840s building had started on all the lower reaches of the hill. On one side the buildings were moving up from Upper North Street through Montpelier Street and Villas, and Victoria Street. Montpelier Crescent was being built on the western edge, and development was moving up Church Street, together with the small terraces going up the eastern side of the hill from the station.

By 1846 only the crown of the hill was left. There were a few early houses in the undeveloped Victoria Road, Clifton Hill and Clifton Road, plus Mr. Vine's Estate and the School House, but apart from these the top of the hill was still sheep down, possibly some farmland and the grounds of the Workhouse on the other side of the Road from Henfield. These had all become isolated, surrounded as they were on the east and south by new houses, and on the west by Montpelier Road, the Temple and the chalybeate spring. The two following engravings illustrate how the natural landscape at the top of the hill changed in the short period between 1823 and 1835.

The first engraving of The Temple in 1823 (discussed more fully in chapter 11) shows the trackway that started life as an unnamed carriage route to the spring from the town, was then referred to as the Road to Blatchington by Kemp and later became Clifton Hill. It runs through fairly open farmland still used for growing corn, with no hedgerows enclosing the fields.

'Ovington near Brighton'
Aquatint drawn and engraved
by William Daniell – 1823.

In the next illustration of the same house, published in 1835 from Horsfield's *History of Sussex*, the artist is standing on the Road from Steyning (now Dyke Road) roughly at the present junction of West Hill Road and Clifton Road, but still portraying much the same view, with early alterations to the Temple having been completed and the many hedgerows having grown up. The trackway in the immediate foreground of the print, with the large hedgerow going downhill from left to right, is the present Dyke Road, and the smaller line of bushes and shrubs in the right hand middle distance marks the present Clifton Hill, with the coach and horses on Montpelier Road just beyond that. The arable field this side of that middle hedgerow is the land on which Clifton Road is later built, and the field on the far side, that stretches up to the house, is the same one as in the previous Daniell print.

A frequent difficulty with the engraving illustrated below is that it was originally published in black and white, so the colouring seen is always a later addition. However, most colourists did not realize that the figures and the child with the hoop are standing on the present Dyke Road, so it should be coloured accordingly – a dust road as in the above illustration. Unfortunately it is usually incorrectly coloured as if it's green fields, as is the case below.

'The Temple Grammar School, Brighton'.
Steel line engraving by H.A. Ogg after G. Earpe
from Horsfield's 'History of Sussex', 1835.

8

The First House on Clifton Hill

Musgrave (1981) records the years 1843 to 1847 for the building of Montpelier Crescent, and Dale (1951) incorrectly records these houses as being the last in Brighton to be designed by A.H.Wilds. In his publication *About Brighton* Dale refers to Park Crescent as being built in 1829, whereas it was actually started in 1849, so it was Park and not Montpelier Crescent that was Wilds' last major undertaking in Brighton. By Kelly's 1846 Post Office Directory, numbers 2 to 27 Montpelier Crescent all have named occupants, and this Directory's introductory description of Brighton paints a lovely picture:

' . . . and on the upper part of the Montpelier Road, a new crescent, built during the past summer; it is a beautiful range of buildings, commanding a view of the hills and low land to the west and north-west, and is called Montpelier Crescent.'

Note the distant small white house on the right hand edge of the following engraving of Montpelier Crescent. This is John Yearsley's home, Clifton Villa, which is mentioned in chapter 6. The fact that the artist could see Yearsley's home in Clifton Hill, rather than the Crescent Inn, the side of which has a completely different elevation, answers questions about the dating of this engraving and the strange angle of the southernmost house in the Crescent. The Crescent is depicted in its early form, before the wings at either end were finished, but the artist has shown the last house on the right to be parallel with Montpelier Road, rather than a continuation of the sweep of the crescent. This is entirely incorrect, and it is likely that this print is nearer 1845 than the c1855 date which usually accompanies its illustration. The suggested 1845 date explains why Yearsley's house can be seen, because the Crescent Inn is not yet built. The print was evidently published before the building of the north and south ends of the Crescent were completed, hence the incorrect depiction of the end house – the artist never saw it. This engraving was very much a tourist and prospective buyer's advertisement, possibly commissioned by A.H. Wilds himself in an effort to secure the development's financial success. It also shows a wall enclosing the private gardens in the front, rather like Hanover Crescent, but there is no evidence of it today. Note the artist's hint in the foreground that traces of the original sheep down still persisted through the building of the Crescent.

'Montpelier Crescent Brighton.'
This print is usually recorded as c1855,
but there are good reasons to date it a decade earlier.
Steel engraving by Newman & Co.
Published by W. Grant, 5 Castle Square.

In the 1830s and early '40s the crescent area was the Temple Fields Cricket Ground, also known as Lee's Trap or Lillywhites (after the famous Brighton cricketing family, who were also noted brickmakers in the town). Bishop (1880) adds some more detail to this area, referring to the ground on which Vernon Terrace is built as being 'for many years used as a nursery garden by Messrs. Parsons and Sons, once well-known florists in the Western-road'. In fact Parsons the nurseryman was occupying that site in Folthorp's 1856 directory, which places his business next door to the Temple, and gave the new residents of the Crescent a delightful outlook. It appears as though his business was on the west side of that part of Montpelier Road that is opposite Denmark Terrace, and extended into the southern part of Vernon Terrace. In this same directory of 1856 can be seen the building of Vernon Terrace, with just numbers 1 to 16 having named occupants, then the usual phrase that accompanies a terrace currently being constructed – 'And other houses unoccupied'. Already numbers 7, 13, 15 and 16 were schools.

The Montpelier Cricket Ground was first used for cricket in 1831, and the area can be seen in the Sickelmore engraving illustrated in chapter 6. It closed in 1844, the building of the Crescent having actually started in 1843. The ground was leased by William Lillywhite from 1836, presumably from T.R. Kemp, and Lillywhite was the proprietor of the Sovereign Inn, Preston Street. Sussex played All England there in 1842 and won by six runs. W.F. Lillywhite was the first player ever to have a benefit match, and according to the *Sussex CCC Handbook* this benefit match was that 1842 Sussex vs. All England game, played on 29, 30th August – the handbook replicates an old window bill. John Yearsley's business partner, Henry Faithfull, is also noted in the Sussex CCC card index as an amateur cricketer who played two matches for Brighton in 1823. There are nine runs to his name. In Squire (1951) there is noted a match between Brighton Amateurs v. Brighton in October 1831, then on 27th June 1833 the Brighton Club played the Trap Club, which included Lillywhite, Lanaway and Brown, and on 25th July of that year there was a match between '22 Gentlemen of Brighton'. In all these entries it is referred to as 'Lees Trap Ground'. From the entry in Squire of 'the Trap Club' it sounds as if this ground had its own local club named after it.

With the closing of the Montpelier ground, one of the most remarkable cricketers of all time, Nicholas Felix, who lived in retirement at 20 Montpelier Street, wrote a sentimental letter to his friend the Earl of Bessborough:

'It is now ten years since I have seen any cricket save what is played by a few small school boys on a ground close at hand, which I suppose was once a field of beautiful green, but now the recipient of material for building purposes. Poor little fellows! Their cricket ground will soon become part of this immense town.' Brodribb (1951).

Apart from being a brilliant left-handed batsman, Felix had invented a bowling machine and initiated the use of India-rubber batting gloves during an illustrious career with Surrey and then Kent (Cricinfo internet site, accessed 2007).

Bearing in mind this date of the mid 1840s for the building of Montpelier Crescent, this gives an approximate date to the Crescent Inn of Clifton Hill, which seems first to appear in the 1846 Directory. Prior to 1844/45, there was no Crescent for the Inn to be named after. It has been suggested that the Inn was the first building on the road to Blatchington. Clifton Villa obviously preceded it by about a year, but in fact the present 13 Clifton Hill was the first house to have been built, by seven or eight years. In the 1876 Directory, the owners of dwellings in Clifton Hill are listed, from number 1, up through the

Crescent Inn which is listed as 6 – Clifton Villa is 7 (as it is today). The list then moves on up to 13, which it calls 'Lone Cottage'. This cottage (Mrs. Watts's laundry of 1839) has been mentioned in chapter 6, as being in Clifton Hill when it was owned by the dairyman C. Thomas and listed in an 1850 Directory, but with no number. So between them the Directories of 1850 and 1876 identify Mrs. Watts's Lone Cottage as the present 13 Clifton Hill, which is the house directly in front of Clifton Mews. With some structural changes, for which there is internal evidence, the picture in Mrs. Watts's advertisement in Leppard's 1839 Directory is this present house.

An internal inspection of number 13 (see illustrations on the following two pages) drew the following conclusions. The present number 13 was originally a double fronted cottage of only single room depth, as the advertisement illustration suggests. The back rooms of the present house are on a different level, two steps up from the front rooms. From brickwork in the loft it can be seen that at some stage the house had a double gabled roof, with a central gully parallel with the front. The oldest parts of the side walls are made of chalk blocks with lime and gravel mix. If the cottage was extended backwards, (after the advertisement illustration) this roof arrangement would have been the obvious result of adding the back rooms. At the rear of the cellar, which is only under the front rooms of the present house, there is a very substantial and early chalk wall, which would have been the back exterior wall if the building was only single room depth originally.

As can be seen in the 1839 advertisement, the house was formerly flat-fronted, but today it has two bays. Again, in the cellar, at the front of the house, there is an old and substantial chalk-built straight wall, not quite to the ceiling of the cellar now, a few inches beyond which there is later brick-work that makes up the present front wall and incorporates the bays. These two walls, at back and front of the cellar, represent the original, single room deep, flat fronted, Lone Cottage. The back was extended, giving rise to a double gabled roof, and a new decorated, bay-fronted front wall was added. In the back garden of this house a hole appeared in the mid 1980s, revealing steps down to an old brick archway. Outside the back door the architect for the modern renovation, the late Paul Briault, told the owners that he had found an angled flight of stone steps going away from the back wall of the house, down into a cellar. These would have been an interior staircase in one of Mrs. Watts' outbuildings. All this indicates buildings, with cellars, behind the original house, as shown in the Leppard advertisement, and is more evidence that the present 13 Clifton Hill was the original Lone Cottage.

Because of its isolation on the carriage track that led to Blatchington the only directions needed to find it were 'top of Montpelier Road', as the advertisement describes. Travelling up Montpelier Road in 1839, having passed the Temple on your left, the only house in the near distance on your right was Lone Cottage, making it the oldest house on the Road to Blatchington, and the first house on Clifton Hill. At this date, the late 1830s, Lone Cottage, together with the Vine estate which had been built some 14 years earlier on Mill Place later Vine Place, while being the only house on what became Clifton Hill, was not the only development on the crown of Church Hill west side. Walking south from Lone Cottage, across the open fields farmed by William Acton where the Powis Estate was later built, plots of land on what was to become Victoria Road had already been sold and two houses built by 1838. Also, while Lone Cottage does not appear to be in any earlier directories, the 1839 illustration does portray it as a well established laundry business, with considerable work buildings behind the front family accommodation. Maybe it had been there for a year or two already? It pre-dates the Crescent Inn by six or seven years, while the trade buildings and commercial activities behind this house give rise to Clifton Mews itself as a business area throughout the early Victorian era, and before the rest of the Clifton/Powis residential development took place. So the Mews was not built at the same time as the Inn, to service it, but was simply converted, probably from the dairyman's business, to serve as the new inn's livery stable.

House number 13 is no longer detached today. It is joined to 15 Clifton Hill by a flying freehold, but it was detached prior to number 15 being rebuilt in the 1980s, and as such it held a strange position in the road. A terrace of four attractive houses, two with ironwork balconies and verandahs, runs up to it from the west, then a carriageway into the Mews, and the detached house itself set further back from the road than this first terrace. Then there was a passageway on the eastern side, and finally a continuing terrace of bay fronted houses, some of which can be dated to 1859 from the deeds to number 16. The reason for the face-lift to the front of this house would have been cosmetic for the area. By the 1850s it was an up and coming, desirable part of town, with decorated, some canopied, bay-fronted homes being built and sold – a flat-fronted, chalk-built tradesman's cottage would have started to look out of place. Re-fronting early houses was a not uncommon Victorian building practice. This present house 13 is the only one in the area with the same double-fronted configuration of door, windows and chimney as the Lone Cottage illustration, and the lie of the land also fits the identification. In Mrs. Watts's advertisement, the land is shown as dropping away quite sharply from the rear west side of the wash-house buildings, and today the ground level in the Mews is some six or seven feet above the level of the back gardens in Clifton Road.

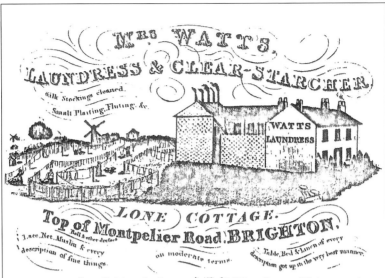

In soliciting the favors of the Nobility, Gentry, Visitors, and Residents, begs most respectfully to inform them that the above Premises—being situated in an open situation, a short distance from the Town, and fitted up with every convenience, together with the advantage of a large field, equal to the country, for drying clothes in—have every thing to recommend them as superior to any other Laundry in the Town for getting-up Linen of every description in the best manner; and that she is, by employing a number of the best hands, enabled to take the Linen of the largest as well as small Families, at the shortest notice, on moderate terms, and pay the most prompt attention and punctuality to their orders.

Mrs. W. begs respectfully to solicit a trial, convinced that the superior manner in which every article entrusted to her care is got up and sent home, will ensure both satisfaction and recommendation.

References of the highest respectability can be given.

The 'Lone Cottage' advertisement in Leppard's 1839 Directory.
To the left of the house can be seen what Mrs. Watts describes as a 'large field, equal to the country', which land became Clifton Road just six years later. In many deeds up to 1850 the French spelling 'Montpellier' is the norm, but this advertisement appears to be a very early exception, using the anglicized spelling.

Lone Cottage as it is today – 13 Clifton Hill, at the front of Clifton Mews.

On an 1875 map in Hove Library, Watts's laundry is shown as having moved across Montpelier Road and situated beside Wick Villa, quite close to Goldsmid Road. The Plan Registry office in Brighton tells us that Lone Cottage was called Glen Atholl by 1895, and has a map of the Mews showing a wash-house, various loose-boxes and stalls, three coach houses, a harness room and, in the middle of the Mews' area, a manure pit.

Returning to the 1839 Directory advertisement illustrated on the previous page, the windmill in the distance would have been Hodson's Mill, built on the later location of West Hill Road in 1804. In the list of addresses in this Directory, apart from her 'Top of Montpelier' identification, Mrs. Watts also appears as 'Lone Cottage in Vine Place'. At that time this could also be a reasonable description of her location, bearing in mind that Vine Place would have been the nearest named roadway coming from the east, and that Kemp's will of 1835 could only describe Clifton Hill as 'a road leading to Blatchington'. This also fits with an early identification for Powis Villas being 'Upper part of Vine Place'. In Hove Library is a watercolour map, dated 1844, showing the western side of Montpelier Road. It shows the continuation of Clifton Hill across Montpelier, and names it as 'To Blatchinton' (sic). This part of the road is now Windlesham Avenue. An article in the *Brighton & Hove Herald* in 1907 reported that 'At the suggestion of Mr. Baldwin, the houses in the lower portion of Clifton-hill from Montpelier-road to the borough boundary, are to be named Windlesham-avenue.'

It is strange that the first name for the present Clifton Hill should associate the road with the small farming community at Blatchington, bearing in mind that the 1808 Thomas Marchant map indicates a completely different origin for the road. On this map there are no roads yet built in the Montpelier area, but up Church Hill and branching off the road 'To London by Steyning' is a 'Carriage Road' that leads out of the town, over the hill and direct to the chalybeate spring. This 'Carriage Road' is exactly where Clifton Hill lies today. Once the carriages got past the parish boundary the road took them sharp left, passing by the southern edge of the spring, and continuing on south through the Rev. Scutt's land and down to the seafront. On this same map, just south of the 'Carriage Road' is the 'footpath' that became Vine Place and Victoria Road. By Baxter's 1822 map this 'Carriage Road' takes the same route but is clearly delineated as a more firmly established roadway. However, by this date Montpelier Road is in place, and the journey from town to the spring waters can avoid the difficult climb up Church Hill by going along the seafront and turning up the new Montpelier Road, a much softer incline. By the time Kemp writes his will in 1835 and names Clifton Hill as a 'Road leading to Blatchington', maps of this period have changed its westerly continuation. Once it arrives at the parish boundary it no longer turns left to the spring, but continues straight on towards Blatchington, and it is this destination, rather than the fashionable chalybeate spring, that gave Clifton Hill its first name.

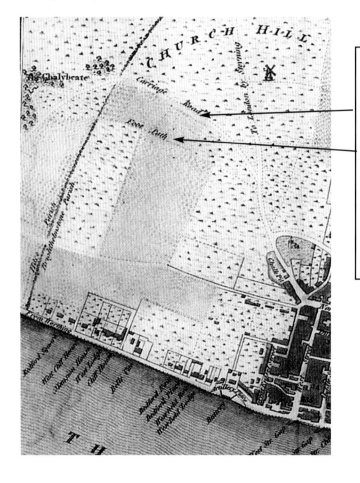

'Survey and Plan of Brighthelmstone' – a detail by Thomas Marchant 1808.

The 'Carriage Road' that became Clifton Hill.

The 'footpath' that became Vine Place and Victoria Road.

The windmill is Hodson's. Vine's Mill was probably built between Marchant's original surveys and the eventual publication date.

Bearing in mind there would not necessarily have been much trade between the windmills of Blatchington and those on Church Hill, Baxter's 1824 *Stranger in Brighton* Directory gives a possible clue as to what may have been the early ecclesiastical origins of the naming of this road from Church-hill to Blatchington, once it ceases to be the primary route to the chalybeate spring. On the subject of St. Nicholas' Church, Baxter writes:

'The living is a vicarage, at present held by Robert James Carr, the very reverend Dean of Hereford. The rectory of West Blatchington, distant about two miles and a half, is annexed to the vicarage, the local church (St. Peter's) having fallen into decay near a century ago.'

At this time St. Andrews church in Hove had also been derelict for many years, and it was not restored for worship until June 1836.

The Rev. Henry Michell Wagner was vicar of Brighton, and of West Blatchington, from 3rd Feb.1825, until his death in 1870. At this time West Blatchington had a population of about 80 souls. The hamlet consisted of a large farmhouse, farm cottages and the unusual windmill, dating from about 1820 and standing as it does on the roof of a barn. And while some of the residents of this small farming community were Quakers, presumably the road from West Blatchington to St. Nicholas' Church (Clifton Hill being the final leg) was much used on a Sunday by those Anglicans who wanted to go to their parish church. Once Montpelier Road was in place, the Road to Blatchington/ Clifton Hill lost its fashionable carriage traffic to the spring waters and became a route that joined this far-flung parishioners' village to their parish church. Sue Berry (2005) adds more details to this joining of the two parishes, noting that the vicar of St. Nicholas' was supported by two livings, which arrangement began when William Colbran, the vicar of Brighton from 1705-1744, also became the rector of West Blatchington in 1712. When he resigned, and to enable his successors to hold both livings, they were legally combined in a deed of union dated 1st August 1744. At this time Brighton just had the one vicar, and every other church in the town apart from St. Nicholas' had either a curate or a priest-in-charge.

Looking at the 1824/25 Pigott-Smith map of the town, and the Marchant one opposite, we can see the sentiment behind the Bartholomews' workhouse inmates objecting to being sent up to their new home on the 'howling wilderness of Church Hill' in 1821. On both maps it is plain how the early residential development of the town extended north up the central valley of the Wellsbourne, west along the coastline into Hove, then up the eastern hill with Edward Street, Carlton Hill and Sussex Street and further up that hill into Brighton Park, later Queens Park. Then the building line went along the eastern seafront, past Royal Crescent to Kemp Town. Amid all this development of the town, Church Hill is deserted into the start of the Victorian era, and the early isolation of Kemp's new home, with the Workhouse, is well illustrated.

Returning to Lone Cottage, the present number 13 was the first house on the Road to Blatchington, and the Leppard illustration is the only known early Victorian image of any house on this road. The logical origins of the three early west to east roads through our particular area also become apparent. Upper North Street started life as the trackway used to get from Hove Village to St. Nicholas' Church. Vine Place and Victoria Road were used as the burial path from the ruined Hove Church to St. Nicholas', and Clifton Hill was eventually used as the route for the parishioners of West Blatchington to get to their parish church. Moving south, on the 1799 Richard Thomas map, the fourth west to east route, Western Road, is included as the 'Foot Way from Hove' leading to Brighton town. As noted in chapter 7, there were no early nineteenth century north to south routes through our area, and the first such roads were between Western Road and Upper North Street.

9

Further Developments and Some Names

Many authors note that between 1820 and 1850 Brighton experienced a faster building and population expansion than any other area in England, despite something of a dip during the middle years. In the final decade Church Hill West Side was no exception to this remarkable growth. Between 1843, when Montpelier Crescent was started, and 1853, when the last terrace of four houses in Powis Villas was completed, this side of Church Hill must have resembled a builder's yard considering the activity that was taking place. Montpelier Crescent was being built, as well as the Crescent Inn (first listed in 1846), while Clifton Mews was being changed from the laundry wash-houses to livery stables. Some of the houses in Clifton Hill were built, plus Powis Villas, Powis Square, the houses on the north side of Victoria Road (some of which had been built a few years earlier) and the whole of Clifton Terrace. The houses were also started at the south end of Clifton Road in 1845. Lower down the hill Montpelier Street was likewise begun in 1845, and Victoria Street was half built by 1850, together with Victoria Place. In addition Robert Gregory notes that in 1850 the houses at the other end of Clifton Road (now Compton Avenue) were also started. Apart from all this activity, 1852-53 saw the rebuilding of St. Nicholas' Church by Richard Cromwell Carpenter, illustrated in chapter 3, when galleries and old high pews were removed, the aisles were widened or lengthened, and major reconstruction of interior and exterior walls was undertaken (Harrison 1931).

All this activity must have been viewed with some amazement by the inmates of the Workhouse, some of whom would undoubtedly have witnessed the whole transformation from sheep down to a small town on a hill – Clifton. Indeed, it is certain that able-bodied men from the Workhouse would have been sent out to work on the building sites to help pay for their keep. Their work would have been the hard graft of digging down into the chalk hillside in preparation for the basements of the new houses. Maybe some found gainful employment and escaped from the Workhouse altogether. In September 1832 the inmates had been given work by the town commissioners on finishing the sea wall on the front, from New Steine to the Royal Crescent. In the same way, when the houses were occupied, some of the women from the Workhouse would have found work as housemaids to their new middle class neighbours and employers.

In January 1857 one young servant girl from the Workhouse, Louisa Abinett, was raped by the master of the house in which she worked. James Bowtell, a shoemaker and father of four, was arrested but later released with just a £10 fine and the Guardians of the Workhouse returned Louisa back into his household (d'Enno 2007). In the mid 1840s there was an average of 120 men in the Workhouse, 194 women and well over 200 children.

This building activity that the inmates witnessed, including almost a 'grandstand' view of the changes to the church, was echoed throughout the town and through later decades. J.G.Bishop (1880) writes:

'Those unacquainted with Brighton in 1850 can scarcely conceive the large area which was covered by bricks and mortar in the subsequent twenty years.'

Gilbert (1954) records that between 1841 and 1871, 7,240 houses were built in Brighton. This mid-nineteenth century period also saw momentous events in the centre of town, with the unfolding of the Pavilion affair, or the Brighton Puzzle as it became known. Between 1846 and 1851 the Pavilion was stripped of its furniture and interior decoration, left as an empty shell, then purchased by the town commissioners, restored and opened with a ball attended by 1,400 guests. This was described as a 'glittering national success' (Dinkel 1993).

In 1854 John Yearsley has his first listing in the Court Section of Taylor's Directory, but this date does not include Williams and Yearsley as ironmongers in the commercial section any longer. The assumption is that not only did Yearsley retire, hence his transfer to the Court listing, but that the business was then sold to Langworthy & Reed, who ran it from 1854 to '64, the name then becoming C & J Reed, who ran it until about 1867.

It is now possible to list the various names, with trades or businesses, that have been found to be involved, not just in new land ownership, but also in the actual building of the Clifton/Montpelier/Powis area. The developers, who were either builders, craftsmen, tradesmen, merchants or professionals, many of whom became residents, known up to the time of publication, were:

Robert Ackerson – builder.
William Baker – china dealer of Brighton.
The Baring family – bankers.
Edward Bruton – stonemason.
John Budgen of Frant – gentleman.

The Rev. Dr. William Henry Butler.

Richard Chapman – stonemason.

Richard Edwards – the co-builder and first occupant of 1 Clifton Terrace. Edwards is listed as both builder and surveyor.

Edward, George and Henry Faithfull – solicitors of 15 Ship Street,

William and Francis Hallett – builders/developers.

John Juniper and Edward Wood – ironmongers of 131 North Street.

John Lewis – Brighton timber merchant.

Richard Patching – builder (died 9th Sept. 1887 aged 82 and buried in Portslade Cemetery) In Baxter's New Brighton Directory of 1822 R. Patching & Son are listed as builders of 26 Duke Street.

Thomas Pelling – carpenter, also listed as bricklayer/plasterer.

William Pierson – butterman.

George David Sawyer and George William Sawyer – carpenters and builders' merchants who ran their carpentry business from Victoria House.

David Sharp – draper of Hurstpierpoint.

Edward Sharp – gentleman,

John Smith – builder.

James Waller – grocer.

Thomas Watts.

William Watts – laundryman.

Fred White – thought to be a builder.

Thomas Willmott – carpenter.

Thomas Wisden – builder and brickmaker – died 2nd December 1871.

John Yearsley – ironmonger, and to a small extent his brother William, a solicitor in Welshpool.

Thomas Young – builder.

Setting the Clifton/Montpelier/Powis development in the town's wider context, in 1866 the West Pier was opened. The top floors of the homes in Powis Square, on the south side, look straight down to this part of the sea-front – indeed the owners could possibly have watched the far end of the pier being built. Four years before this the foundation stone of the Grand Hotel, designed by J. H. Whichcord, was laid. It was opened in 1864, in a blaze of publicity, with all 300 of its rooms taken, and again the top of this building might have been seen from the highest rooms in some of the new Powis homes. Further developmental setting for our estate was the Charter of Incorporation, granted to Brighton on 1st April 1854, the first mayor of Brighton being Lt. Col. John Fawsett. And at the end of the previous decade, just as our development was gathering pace, the townsfolk witnessed the extraordinary spectacle of Queen

Victoria's arrangements for the removal of all the furniture and fittings from the Royal Pavilion. Through 1847-48, no fewer than 143 removal van-loads reduced the Pavilion to an empty shell (Horlock 2005). The Queen used much of what was taken from Brighton to furnish the new front that had been built at Buckingham Palace.

With the emergence of the well-off industrial and business classes in the town, the areas on the hill slopes near the station, and the empty spaces between Brighton and Kemp Town in the east and Brighton and Hove in the west were the ideal building plots for their new homes. But while to the east and the west they typically built imposing terraces of tall three and four storey houses, by contrast the four moderately sized, detached houses that take up the whole of the west side of Powis Villas represent a singular residential development in early Victorian Brighton. They stand today as the remarkable influence of the Welshman John Yearsley and his partners, there being no other early Victorian street like it in the town.

The previously distinct social gulf that Ken Fines (2004) describes, between the gentry and the labouring classes of Brighton, had been filled. The high-earning middle classes had arrived, and these four detached homes in Powis Villas were a unique and definitive statement of their identity. There was of course the fifth detached residence, Aberdeen Lodge, number 5, on the east side and northern corner with Clifton Hill, that was given a grander and more distinctive elevation than the other four, together with an Italianate tower similar to 1 & 2 Clifton Hill. This was the largest villa in Powis. It included the flint barn in its grounds, and its original private garden extended behind numbers 6 and 7, reaching down to a border with Powis Grove. In the rate book of 1854 (ESRO BH/B/4/37/2) this extension to the garden was listed separately under '6 Powis Grove – Joseph Browne, a garden – 2/-'.

Apart from several short terraces, Powis Grove itself also has three detached villas. The two largest houses in Powis Villas, numbers 1 and 5 are not listed in 1850: they first appear in the 1852 street directories. The building plots were obviously marked out in 1850, because at this date the existing houses are already numbered 2, 3 and 4. By 1852 Mr. Thomas Smith lived at 1 Powis Villas, and Mr. Joseph Browne at number 5. They must have been the first owners of these houses: they are both listed in the Directory's Court Section and Mr. Browne's business was statuary and decorative plaster work, which is much in evidence around his home. His flint barn has a sitting lion on the side buttress, four classical head reliefs on the west wall and a large circular relief above these. On the wall posts around the house there are four acorn motifs (presumably there were six originally), and these are unique exterior decorations in the area. Inside his home today there remain three alcoves which were presumably made for statues, and in part of the main hallway there are two long reliefs of Roman charioteers and a large circular decoration of classical figures over a door.

While west-side Powis Villas was Yearsley's development, the north-eastern end was not. It was Vine's land and not included in Yearsley's original purchase. So the houses numbered 5, 6 and 7 had to wait for the mill to be knocked down. Gray suggests that its demolition was in 1848, but if it was this early, there was quite a time lapse before the houses were built this side of Powis Villas. From the directories, early 1850 seems a more likely date for the mill's demise. The land was owned by Edward Cuttress, but it is not known if he sold it to a developer or had a hand in the residential buildings himself. However, the different ownership explains the rather different style of these houses to those on the west side.

This newly built middle class enclave just up the hill from the old town also had enormous health benefits over the late eighteenth and early nineteenth century homes in the town. By the 1840s the drainage and sanitation of Brighton, among many other towns, was beginning to be of concern in London. The 1848 Public Health Act recommended household drainage in place of cesspools, the improvement of household water supplies and the increased provision of public baths. However, the 1825 Act of Parliament regarding the governance of Brighton enabled the town commissioners to lawfully reject these 1848 recommendations, which they formally did in 1850. By the end of November 1860 a series of letters appeared in the *Times*, prompted by a visitor to one of the eastern terraces overlooking the sea at Kemp Town. The gentleman's whole family and servants had been quite ill as a result of what he described as the 'poisonous atmospheric agency', and the fact that the drainage of the house was 'wretchedly imperfect'. Reference was made to a report dated 14th May 1859 by an eminent engineer, Mr. Rawlinson, who wrote that Brighton 'badly wanted drains and sewers'. Further reference was made to a subsequent and more detailed report published by another distinguished civil engineer, Mr. Hawksley.

Hawksley's report of 29th October 1859 makes disgusting reading and was of grave concern to a town that relied on tourism for much of its economy. He wrote:

'I have ascertained that fully three fourths of all the houses in the town are dependent for their drainage upon cesspools, constructed chiefly in the stratum of chalk upon which the dwellings are for the most part erected. The consequences of the system are only less injurious in Brighton than in most other important towns because of the very pervious character . . . . of the natural carbonate of lime of which the chalk is principally composed: but I am nevertheless informed that in many instances the evil effects of this fouling of the substratum, and of pollution of wells by the cesspools, are beginning to be seriously felt . . .' (Brighton & Hove Libraries-on-Line – accessed 2006).

The new mid-nineteenth century homes of Church Hill – West Side would also have relied on wells and cesspools during their early years of occupation, but of course they were new and had not developed the pollution problems of central Brighton where, like other towns and cities, the system had been in use for decades. The wells on the hill would also have had to have been a lot deeper than those of the low lying ground in the town. Clifton Mews would have had wells with a substantial water supply as a legacy from Mrs. Watts's laundry business of the late 1830s, and no doubt in the 1820s the inmates of the new Workhouse had to dig a well which would have been made available to its later residential neighbours. In addition, Folthorp's 1856 Directory carried advertisements by the Brighton, Hove and Preston Water Company, with their office in Bond Street. They first obtained their supply 'by means of a steam-engine, which pumps up water from the depth of 100 feet, the reservoir of which is on the west-side of Race-hill,' (Fleet 1847) and they advertised water for delivery for domestic use at a cost of '9d in the Pound' – a welcome alternative if your own household well was contaminated. To emphasize the contrast at this time between the poverty of some parts of central Brighton and what J.G.Bishop in chapter 2 described as the 'handsome and fine property' of Church Hill, Clifford Musgrave's *Life in Brighton* (1981) is a good reference. Musgrave quotes from a guide book, *Brighton As It Is*, written by a graduate of London University in 1860, in which the houses of the poor in the town centre are described. These homes were 'situated in narrow streets . . . ill-ventilated, badly drained if at-all . . . built with inferior bricks and mortar made of sea-sand . . . wretchedly damp so that even the walls are covered with lichen'. But half a mile away up the hill, our new houses had the modern luxury of gas lighting available to them, unpolluted water supplies and drainage that had not yet caused problems. No wonder the homes on Church Hill engendered thoughts of 'The West End of town'. The corporation finally took control of the water supply in 1872, and a plan from a private Powis Square deed dated August 1873 shows the position of the new drains connecting to the main sewer, (cmpca news 9).

In chapter 7 it was mentioned that Yearsley's youngest daughter, Julia, married the son of R.P.B. Taaffe. This Richard P.B. Taaffe, M.D., qualified in London, was one of the founders of the first Children's Hospital in 1868, taking over a private house at 178 Western Road, and was one of its first two acting physicians. He was also one of the surgeons to the Sussex and Brighton Eye Infirmary in Queen's Road. Due to increasing demand, the unit in Western Road had to buy the house next door in 1870, and later that year the governing body of the hospital purchased the one and a quarter acres of land referred to as 'Church Hill School House Estate' (where the Royal Alexandra Hospital for children stood until 2007, on the north eastern corner of Clifton Hill and Dyke

Road). The school house building was officially opened as a children's hospital by the Bishop of Chichester on July 14th 1871. New foundations were laid in 1880, and the Royal Alexandra Hospital on Dyke Road was opened in July 1881. The hospital building was designed by Thomas Lainson (1825–1898), a prolific local architect who was also responsible for the Middle Street Synagogue, the house that became Hove Museum and the large red-brick warehouse in Holland Road, together with many private homes in the city. Richard Taaffe, Julia Yearsley's father-in-law, and by then the first appointed medical officer of health for Brighton, gave his name to Taaffe ward on the ground floor. His photograph was published in the *Brighton Times* of 23rd June 1882 in that paper's monthly series of 'Local Celebrities'. This article also included some interesting details of the opening of the hospital. The ceremony was performed by their royal highnesses the Prince and Princess of Wales, accompanied by the young princesses, on July 21st 1881. During the ceremony Dr. Taaffe 'presented the Prince with a gold key which accurately fitted the lock of the principal door of the building'. The key was in the Queen Anne style, about three inches long. The report goes on:

'It is believed that this was the first instance of presenting a gold key to Royalty at the opening of a building, and the example has since been followed in Leicester and Yarmouth . . . Before leaving the hospital Dr. Taaffe asked permission to be allowed to name the hospital the Royal Alexandra Hospital, to which request a most gracious assent was accorded. This was the first occasion on which the Young Princesses appeared at a public ceremony.'

From 'The Graphic' – 1881, with the caption, 'The Prince and Princess visiting one of the wards'.

Both this and the next illustration are woodcuts by J.R.Brown, and this is the only known engraving depicting the interior of the hospital.

Naming the hospital thus not only celebrated the visit of the Princess of Wales herself, but two of the three princesses also had the Christian name of Alexandra. When the hospital finally left its site in 2007, this triangle of land, which started life as a soap manufactory, had been associated with the welfare of Brighton's children, in their education or their health, for 185 years. The naming of the piece of land as

'Church Hill School House Estate' in the hospital records is interesting. There are no maps with this piece of land so named, but on the maps available, dating from 1822 onwards, there is always an unnamed building on this triangle of land and, as will be shown, May 1822 was the date the school was founded.

A past vicar of St. Nicholas' confirmed that in the last century there was a church school, but the records were not in his possession. The deeds of 16 Clifton Hill confirm the Rev. William Henry Butler LLD. owned that triangle of land in 1843 and Kelly's 1846 Brighton Directory confirms his involvement with a school on that site – the listing for Church hill reads, 'Rev. William Henry Butler D.C.L. – Church hill boarding school'. It was a boys' school and is still listed in Folthorp's 1850 Directory, together with the Workhouse and Infirmary. It would certainly have educated children from the Workhouse, bearing in mind that the school was established many years before much residential development had taken place in its vicinity.

The *Brighton Herald* of 3rd May 1845 reported that in the first quarter of that year the Workhouse was home to 232 children. However, with the 1846 directory referring to the Church Hill 'boarding' school, presumably a certain age-range of the boys lived at the school, while still being registered at the Workhouse.

The Children's Hospital as illustrated in 'The Graphic' on July 30th 1881, in an article recording the visit to Brighton of The Prince and Princess of Wales.

Prior to the Church Hill building, the original eighteenth century Workhouse, or poor-house, had been built in 1733 on the site of a chapel belonging to a convent of friars who lived on alms and served the poor (note 6).

This first poor-house is often said to have been erected by the Prior of St. Pancras, Lewes, and dedicated to St. Bartholomew (Saunders 1837), hence the 'Bartholomews' area in the town today. Aitchison (1926) writes that this Priory of St. Bartolomew was probably destroyed during a French raid on the town, but casts doubt on its association with the Cluniac Prior of Lewes, 'one of the great men of the country', and far removed in spirit from the alms-living Brighton friars serving the poor. The Directors and Guardians of the Poor then bought land on Church Hill and built a new Workhouse in 1821. Dale (1976) describes its total cost as nearly £5,000, whereas Martin (1871) records the cost as £10,000, 'in addition to £1,600 for the land (between 13 and 14 acres) purchased in 1818 and paid for by a rate made expressly for that purpose'. As can be seen from various maps, its location was on the northern edge of St. Nicholas's northern graveyard, in that part of Dyke Road opposite where the turnings to Clifton Terrace and Powis Grove are now placed, with the foundation stone being laid by the vicar, the Rev. Dr. Carr.

The Workhouse grounds are now covered by Buckingham Road, Alexandra Villas and Albert Road. When the Workhouse was first built on Church Hill the inmates of the original one in the town did not want to be moved, as Erredge wrote, 'out of the world . . . and into the howling wilderness of Church Hill'. Besides the church, Shelley's cottage, and Mr. Vine's small estate, there were few other buildings on Church Hill in 1820, when the Workhouse was commenced (Erredge 1862). Contrary to Martin (1871) Erredge wrote that the Workhouse had about nine acres of land, partly for vegetables and grazing for sheep according to the Nibbs lithograph illustrated in chapter 2, with the obligatory Infirmary building established few yards to the north.

A previously erected building, across the road from the Workhouse, was a candle and soap manufactory, run by Mr. Edward Heard. His business failed, and it was these premises that became the Church Hill School, started by the Rev. Thomas Airey. He was succeeded by the Rev. Dr. Butler, who was followed by the Rev. Pugh, and it was this cleric who eventually sold the site for the new Children's Hospital. Airey had entered into a lease agreement with Kemp for this triangle of land on 9th May 1822. The price was £150 for a 14 year lease (ESRO SASDD/647).

The following year Airey agreed to buy the property (ESRO HOW/118/2) (note 7). Interestingly, the site originally bought for the hospital in 1870 is noted in their deeds as being one and a quarter acres. When it came up for auction in 2006 the site was advertised as being 1.72 acres, so in 136 years the hospital complex itself had managed only a small expansion of its land holdings on the hill. It had of course expanded on the other side of Clifton Hill by buying residential properties in Powis Villas.

The candle and soap business run by Edward Heard, which preceded the children's arrival on this site, is an interesting story. In the ESRO AMS 6468/3 document he is described as a 'practical chemist' who employed a hydraulic press for the separation of the constituents of fat for candle making. The documents report that Mr. Heard was 'using a more powerful pressure than that used by the French Chemists . . . and produced a substance of a beautiful appearance which made candles possessing all the desirable qualities of a wax light at one half the expense. He obtained for this discovery Patents for the Three Kingdoms in the year 1819, and had extensive works erected on the Church Hill at Brighton for their manufacture. Here he produced candles, Cocoa Nut and Palm oils; and made soaps with the separated oil. Considerable encouragement was given to this new fabric at Brighton, London and other parts of the Kingdom; but a most distressing state of health and crippled resources, which precluded a supply equal to public demand, at length obliged (Mr. Heard) to give up the establishment and remove from that part of the country. Mr. Heard resumed the candle trade in London, and took out a fresh patent in 1829.' This document implies that Heard gained his patent in 1819 and without delay built his premises on Church Hill, on land leased from Kemp. His business lasted from 1819 probably to the spring of 1822. The Rev. Airey then bought the premises from the distressed Mr. Heard and renegotiated the lease from Kemp.

Returning to the Grove Villa deeds, they tell us that Mr. & Mrs. R.J.C. Taaffe (that is, the youngest daughter Julia Yearsley and her husband) became the owners of Grove Villa on July 3rd 1876. They owned the house until 26th January 1920, when it was sold to Mr. M. Dampier, but there is no evidence of the Taaffes ever living there. R.J.C.Taaffe was a member of Lincoln's Inn, called to the Bar in 1876, and a member of the South Eastern Circuit. In Page's 1879 Directory the widow Yearsley is still listed as living in Grove Villa, and she is also still listed in the Court Section as being in 4 Powis Villas (by this time the directories seem to have dropped the 23 Clifton Hill duplication). At this same date, R.P.B. Taaffe MD. of the Old Steine is also listed, but there is no other Taaffe noted as living in Brighton.

Since this is the final house that John Yearsley built for his own family, it seems appropriate to list its residents through the years. After Julia Yearsley, the occupants were Mrs. Coomber to 1900, A.G. Sharman to 1905 and W.T. Dewe to 1910, who presumably all rented it from Mr. & Mrs. Taaffe. Maud and Mary Sleigh and the Misses Dampier rented it throughout the First World War, then Mr. M. Dampier purchased the house from Taffee in 1920, perhaps for his spinster sisters to live there. By 1938 Miss M.E. Dampier was the sole occupant, and there is no record of Mr. M. Dampier the purchaser ever living there. A final reference to Gray's notes, which earlier introduced us to John Yearsley of Powysland, is tantalizing:

'My wife's grandfather, who was born in Brighton in 1852 and who died in 1938, was apprenticed in the building trade in 1866 and spent all his life in that trade. He informs me that the same man (meaning the actual builder) built numbers 6 to 13 in Montpelier Terrace, all 20 houses in Montpelier Villas, and 10 to 13 Powis Villas, in the space of about ten years. The name of the builder is not known to me.'

So near yet so far from knowing the name of the actual builder of one of the most delightful streets in Brighton and Hove, Montpelier Villas, which, in the *Guide to the Buildings of Brighton* (Robson and Macdonald 1987), is described as being the later work of A.H. Wilds. Having used Gray for many details of early land dealings on Church Hill, it is good to see that his notes, with just a few inaccuracies, are in the historical tradition of personal conversations handed down through the generations.

To speculate on who did build all these houses that Gray mentions, in that particular decade and in this area, the builder who had the financial resources, and the man-power needed was William Hallett. The same speculation could apply regarding who Wilds employed for the construction of Montpelier Crescent, an enormous undertaking completed in the short space of four years, bearing in mind all the delays that winter weather might have caused.

10

The Southern Limits – Towards the Sea

The names of Clifton, Montpelier and Powis on Church Hill – West Side are situated such that Clifton and Powis are compact areas on the top of the hill. The name of Montpelier on the other hand stretches the entire western length of the estate, from the Seven Dials down to the seafront, with its namesake roads placed along the southern edge, in Montpelier Villas, Street, then Terrace and Montpelier Place. The Villas and the Street were built on the northern side of North Street Road, now Upper North Street running into Montpelier Terrace, the original trackway used to get from Hove Village to St. Nicholas' Church in the early 1800s.

Along this route, apart from the tiny beer house that became the Windmill Inn, the earliest home on this southern part of the hill appears to be Hampton Villa, 14 Montpelier Terrace. As streets and roads developed through the early Victorian period, there were inevitable name and number changes, and Hampton Villa, built at the beginning of William IV's reign, is an extreme example of this, having ten different addresses in its first twenty years. It was built by 1832, when in the List of Electors to the Whalesbone 100, its situation was described as Hampton Villa, 76 Western Road and the first resident and presumed owner was John Bradshaw, a tailor, (Doyne-Ditmas 2000). John Bradshaw is listed as a tailor at 4 Castle Square in 1822. By Baxter's 1824 Directory his business is at 97 St. James's Street, and by the 1832 Brighton Directory he is trading as J. & J. Bradshaw, tailors of 75 Western Road. This 1832 listing of Hampton Villa at 76 Western Road, and Bradshaw's business at 75 Western Road at the same date suggests either that he ran his business from his new home or that his shop was just on the corner of Hampton Place and Western Road. In the 1840 Burial Ground Rate Book (ESRO BH/B/4/34/1) the house is listed under the entry for Hampton Place, which has 31 numbered houses, with Bradshaw in Hampton Villa listed as number 16, paying a rate of six shillings. Bradshaw also signed the Poor Rate Book for 1844 as one of St. Nicholas' churchwardens (ESRO BH/B/4/35/2).

The date of the early 1830s for Hampton Villa ties in with the early developments along Upper North Street, and gives a strong clue as to the builder of this house. In chapter 5 the deeds to number 88 in this street were mentioned. These recorded that in June 1830 Kemp sold a tract of land on this north side of Upper North Street to William and Francis Hallett, and that William built number 88 and sold it in 1837. The tract of land also included 1 Hampton Terrace and the next door house is Hampton Villa, so it is reasonable to assume that its land was also in the Hallett purchase of 1830. Because the first owner of Hampton Villa in 1832 was Bradshaw the tailor, and not another builder who could have bought the plot from Hallett and built on it, the most obvious builder of Hampton Villa was William Hallett himself, and it seems to be one of the first houses he built after his original purchase from Kemp. In 1832 Hallett is listed as living at 7 Hampton Place, just a few yards down the hill from the Villa. Number 7 is number 18 today: it has the largest garden in the street, with an outbuilding which was probably a store house for Hallett's business. Hallett built this whole central section of the east side of Hampton Place, which today runs from 14 to 26, for the developer Edward Patzcker from Poole, at much the same time he built Bradshaw's new home and then the smaller Hampton Terrace. What is certain is that Codrington was not involved in this development, as his land holdings did not extend north of Codrington House itself. On the next illustrated map, published in 1836 by William Wallis, Hampton Place is just dotted lines, with the implication that this road was still an on-going development. But Wallis was a London publisher, which helps to explain a couple of years gap between drawing and the actual publication, and why Wallis fails to portray the road with the well developed terraces that it had by the mid 1830s.

A resident of Hampton Place, Mick Hamer, has researched the history of his home, and put together the following details. This Edward Patzcker just mentioned was a ship owner and timber merchant based in the port of Poole. In February 1829 he married a wealthy widow, Mrs. Margaret Wanhill, and shortly after purchased a plot of land on the east side of Hampton Place, although his connections with Brighton are unknown. Possibly as early as 1829/30 he either employed or partnered William Hallett to build the central section of Hampton Place, the present numbers 14 to 26. Hallett built number 7 for himself, and made it the largest home in this section. In an auction advertisement in the *Times*, 23rd March 1839, it is described as having an extra drawing room, opening to a conservatory, and a large walled garden. The property also included a builder's yard, accessed from 'Back-street, with workshops, saw-pit, sheds, etc' – much the same arrangement as the Sawyers created behind Victoria House a couple of years later. Patzcker then had financial difficulties and in March 1836 borrowed £4,000 at 4.5% interest from Patrick Hadow, a London stockbroker. He made at least two auction attempts to redeem this mortgage. The first was advertised in the *Times* on 27th June

1836, with the terrace described as 'seven capital newly-finished houses in Hampton Place, and commodious builder's yard and workshops in Back-street', all let and producing an annual income of £348. 10s. This unsuccessful sale was handled by one agent, Mr. A. Murray of 47 Parliament Street, Westminster. In the second auction of March 1839, referred to earlier, Patzcker spread a wider net, and the sale was offered through Mr. Weller of 29 Essex Street, London, W.E. Weddall of Gosport and Messrs. Webb, land agents of 1 Marine Parade, Brighton. Patzcker was declared bankrupt in May 1837, and after the second failed auction the houses became the property of Mr. Hadow, and stayed in his family until 1904. Clearly Hallett never owned his home at number 7, but maybe he had advantageous terms to his lease. Patzcker later took the position of Prussian vice consul to the port of Poole, which he held for at least ten years. It was a title grander than the reality, but gives a clue that the man himself might have come from Berlin or its surrounds.

The section of houses immediately south of Patzcker's terrace was built at much the same time, possibly completed a few months earlier. In the Guildhall Library (MS 11936-523) are insurance documents from the Sun Fire Office for number 4 Hampton Place, now number 10. The policy is for the year 1830–31, the policy holder is Thomas Alfred Powell, wine merchant of 3 King Court, Lombard Street, London, and his tenant in Hampton Place is Mr. Deacon. For a premium of 18 shillings the house is insured for £450, a 'stable in yard near' insured for £50 and 'coach house and dwelling room over' for £100. These last two properties were in Hampton Street. Also in Hampton Street at this time was William Murrell, listed as 'cow keeper and dairyman'. Murrell is mentioned in chapters 2 and 4 in connection with New England Farm, and Clifton Gardens Mill. In 1832 another resident was Sir George Head (1782 – 1855), who lived at number 2, now 8 Hampton Place. After an international career in the army he acted as deputy knight-marshall at the coronation of William IV, for which he was knighted on 12th October 1831. He went on to hold the same position to Queen Victoria.

As noted earlier, the Windmill Inn was the first building on the then unnamed track that became Upper North Street, and presumably rebuilt in 1828 when it received its full licence. Julia Doyne-Ditmas notes the striking similarities between the Inn and Hampton Villa, in terms of corner position, size, their original roof line and door and window configurations. Hampton Villa had the same slate roof as the Inn, before a roof garden replaced it in the early 1980s. The possibility is that William Hallett, or maybe his father Francis, was involved with the rebuilding of the Inn in 1828. A couple of years later Bradshaw commissions William Hallett to build a home and business premises for him just a few yards to the west, and the design of the relatively new Inn turns out to be an acceptable choice for both builder and client.

Hampton Villa in 2007   The Windmill Inn in 2007

A decade earlier this part of Western Road was called Western Place, with the section nearer the centre of town called Regent Place. The villa being named Hampton at this time connects it with Hampton Lodge, the first 'Hampton' in the area, actually on Western Road, and then Hampton Place joined the Villa with Hampton Lodge. Carder (1990) suggests 1823 for the building of Hampton Lodge, but according to documents from 34 Sillwood Road it was there in the summer of 1822, and this date is confirmed on W. Belch's 1822 map illustrated in chapter 1. Carder also describes it as a house and then writes that it can still be seen behind the single storey shops built along Western Road in 1903. In fact it was a bungalow, from the illustration in chapter 7, and the site has now been completely rebuilt into the two four storey houses, numbers 139 and 140 Western Road, which match the height of the Codrington houses on either side.

The earliest document (private collection) from the land on which 34 Sillwood Road was later built is dated 17th August 1822 and is a restrictive covenant established by Fauntleroy. It prohibits Ann Sober and her heirs or assigns from building anything which would 'become a nuisance to Henry Fauntleroy, or in anywise obstruct the present view or prospect from the dwellinghouse occupied by the said Henry Fauntleroy on the north side of Western Place Road'. It further restricted Mrs. Sober from establishing any businesses on the piece of land she owned immediately south of Hampton Lodge, but she could plant tress and shrubs. This covenant would have been included in all the deeds to the large Victorian houses on the west side of Sillwood Road, which run from Sillwood Terrace down to the start of the smaller homes from number 31. These large homes, with ironwork balconies and verandahs, were begun in 1870 and completed by 1875.

After Fauntleroy's death a second restrictive covenant was imposed, presumably by Codrington as the next owner of Hampton Lodge. This was dated 15th April 1831 (private collection) and it stipulated that if Mrs. Sober had plans for development of the gardens to the south of her own home, she could only build detached villas or a terrace of one unified design. In the end she did neither.

Both these restrictive covenants, 1822 and 1831, seem to have missed the boat as far as Western Cottages was concerned. It is known that Constable stayed in Western Cottages, as a guest of Mrs. Sober, in 1824, and it seems reasonable that his oil painting of 'Gothic House and Western Lodge, Brighton' was painted as the view from his front room. This picture is dated August 1824, but the cottages must have been there by August 1822, or the covenant from Fauntleroy would have prohibited them from being built. As it was, in 1822, the view directly south from Hampton Lodge was already restricted to a gap between Western Lodge itself, to the right of the view, and Western Cottages to the left – although, by the lie of the land, Fauntleroy may well have just managed a sea view over the roofs of the cottages. The map of the area published in 1822 and illustrated in chapter 1, shows the large houses north and south of our Western Road, but does not have Western Cottages in place. This map must have been drawn during 1821, so further suggests 1822 as the building date for the first section of the cottages, and indeed Fauntleroy's 1822 restrictive covenant may have been in direct response to Mrs. Sober's development of this terrace, which seriously affected the view south from Hampton Lodge.

In the 1840 rate book at the ESRO (refs. given) the terrace of Western Cottages is referred to as Western Buildings and it has numbers 1 to 18 with Mrs. Sober owning number 8. It is her ownership of number 8 that confirms we are looking at the same group of houses. By the 1844 rate book the entry reads 'Western Buildings', but with the word 'Buildings' crossed through and 'Cottages' written in its place, and the numbers have extended up to 31. So between 1840 and 1844 the original 18 cottages were extended on down the road, and a short way back up the other western side to where 31 is today. This western side of the road would be encroaching on Mrs. Sober's original gardens which is probably why only a short section was developed, with the remainder left until the 1870 development. This confusion over the name Western 'Cottages' or 'Buildings' is explained in the privately held deeds to 14 Sillwood Road. A lease agreement on that house, dated 13th March 1835, refers to the house as '12 Western Buildings but now identified as 14 Western Cottages'. Further deeds at the ESRO (ACC8745/44), showing transactions between 1850 and 1855, also record this name change, listing '18-20 Western Cottages (formerly 6-7 Western Buildings)', and '21-25 Western Cottages (formerly 9-13 Western Buildings) Brighton'. The first noted record of the name change, in the 1835 lease, makes the 1840 and '44 rate books seem a little late in catching up with the alteration, and of course it is not clear from the 1835 lease when this change took place. When Constable was a guest of Mrs. Sober in the summer of 1824 the road was called Western Cottages, so it only spent the first couple of years of its existence as Western Buildings. These deeds to 14 Sillwood

Road refer to Mrs. Sober's title to her land and list it as 'in the furlong next West Fields in the West Laine part of 10 pauls formerly Gunn's'. The deeds then mention Thomas Friend's will, dated 6th March 1761, in which he leaves to his nephew, also called Thomas Friend, 'land, farm, barn, buildings, tenements and holdings in Brighton, also called the priory, which he purchased from William Shadwell'. These names of Gunn and Shadwell are noted in chapter 1 as early eighteenth century landowners in the town. In the mid 1840s, while Mrs. Sober was the owner of number 8, Edward Codrington owned numbers 1 and 2. His ownership may explain why permission had been granted to build more dwellings at the southern end of Western Cottages, and the earlier covenants had obviously not been adhered to – Codrington was the owner of Hampton Lodge by this time, and as such had the power to overturn them. These two houses at numbers 1 and 2 were valued in the Codrington Estate in 1884 at £1,080 each, and by then were referred to as Sillwood Road. However, in that valuation the much larger Codrington House itself was only valued at £1,850, so maybe Codrington had the two small original late Georgian Western Cottages developed into larger premises, which were in turn knocked down to make way for the present bank building. An alternative explanation is that the original terrace of cottages did not reach all the way up to our present Western Road, and there was an undeveloped plot of land at the top end on which Codrington built his two houses. This would account for one of the changes in numbering, when house 12 became number 14.

Referring back to Thomas Friend's will of March 1761 in the deeds to 14 Sillwood Road, this is quite a complicated document, ensuring that all this farmland remained in the family for future generations. His nephew, the second Thomas Friend, was left a life interest in the land, with the reversionary interests under the control of Nicholas Willard and Thomas Marcham, although these two gentlemen had no rights to the land in question. The will then left the life interest to the male heir of this second Thomas Friend, but when he died without children the life interest passed to his nephew John Kemp, who as noted in chapter 1 died childless in September 1774. The next in line to inherit was John's younger brother, George Kemp, but he predeceased John, and so the land passed to George's eldest son, Thomas Kemp – Thomas Read Kemp's father. So T.R. Kemp's final ownership of much of Brighton rested on events of an unlikely combination – two early relatives having no children, and a younger brother dying before his elder brother.

Another of the documents to number 14 mentions an indenture dated 18th April 1771, naming Thomas Kemp as the 'tail-male', which brought to an end the reversionary interests of Willard and Marcham, bestowed all interests in the land on Thomas Kemp and was an eighteenth century legal arrangement which ensured the preservation of the family assets. This same document then quotes agreements for the following day, 19th April 1771, between Thomas Kemp, John Ellis (who was required to be 'a perfect tenant'), Walter Windsor, gent, and John Kemp. The next entry has the interesting date of 'Easter Term 11th Geo 3rd' which means the April or May of 1771. It refers to Thomas Kemp as John Ellis's 'vouchee' and then lists the property that is described as 'The Manor of Erlyes'. Presumably part of the property listed is in the West Laine but, as will be seen, it goes beyond Brighton. The list is – '10 messuages, 4 (stables?), 2 Dove Houses, 4 gardens, 320 acres of land, 30 acres of meadow, 700 acres of pasture, 50 acres of Furze and Heath, 1 acre covered with water, with appurtenances in Brighton, Edburton, otherwise Aberton, St. Michael's Lewes and St. John under the Castle of Lewes'.

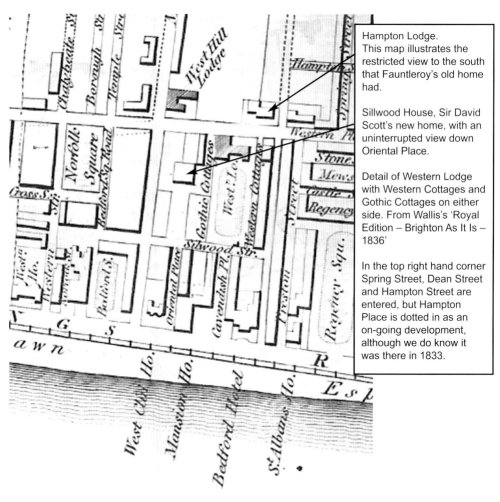

Hampton Lodge. This map illustrates the restricted view to the south that Fauntleroy's old home had.

Sillwood House, Sir David Scott's new home, with an uninterrupted view down Oriental Place.

Detail of Western Lodge with Western Cottages and Gothic Cottages on either side. From Wallis's 'Royal Edition – Brighton As It Is – 1836'

In the top right hand corner Spring Street, Dean Street and Hampton Street are entered, but Hampton Place is dotted in as an on-going development, although we do know it was there in 1833.

This deed then moves on to 17th/18th July 1771 and introduces the proposed marriage of Thomas Read Kemp's future parents. There is an indenture of '5 parts' between John and Thomas Kemp, Henry Read Esq and John Bean, gent, Anne Read, spinster, Henry Read the younger and Henry Earl, and finally Thomas Land Esq and Francis Whisseld. The indenture then reads, 'After reciting that a marriage was intended between the said Thomas Kemp and the said Anne Read – It was witnessed that in consideration of the said intended marriage and of £4,000 to Thomas Kemp, paid by Henry Read the elder, and £6,000 to be paid within 12 months of Henry Read's death'. So these deeds to 14 Sillwood Road seem to begin by quoting land in the West Laine, but widen their frame of reference to include details of the original agreement that saw much of Brighton and its surrounds fall into the hands of Thomas Read Kemp's father, Thomas Kemp, once his uncle John Kemp had died in 1774 and he married the spinster Anne Read.

In the 1845 rate book Mrs. Sober is listed as the owner of numbers 8, 16 and 17 Western Cottages, and by 1854 she had dispensed with numbers 16 and 17, having previously rented them to Catherine Grigen and Elizabeth Lancaster. Many of the houses that now form the east side of Sillwood Road are still being quoted in the street directories as Western Cottages in the late 1860s, so it appears that the Sillwood Road name was adopted when the large Victorian houses opposite were started in 1871.

As Western Cottages developed it did not remain an exclusively residential road. In the 1846 Post Office Directory it included five lodging houses, two fly-proprietors, a boot and shoe maker, a coal merchant and a Servants' Institution at number 25. Behind Western Cottages was Little Preston Street, which had six listed addresses in the 1840 rate book. There was a mixture of shops and stables, with number 6 being a real-tennis court owned by Hall & Co.

At this date Preston Street itself had 83 listed premises, together with a number of undeveloped plots. There was a variety of private houses, shops with homes above, stables and a bakehouse, while number 119 was a billiard room owned by Frederick Mahomed.

On the west side of Western Lodge and Mrs. Sober's gardens, during the early 1840s, Western Terrace had numbers 1 to 8, with A.H. Wilds at 5. In the 1845 rate book the numbers have changed and become 2 to 9, and Wilds is listed as owning the whole terrace. In the 1836 map, illustrated above, Western Terrace is entered as 'Gothic Cottages', which was presumably the name that Wilds and Busby first gave it while they were building the Gothic House. In Constable's 1824 painting of Western Lodge, the Gothic House is close to the western edge of the Lodge's gardens, and has wooden scaffolding around it, a ladder towards the left of the façade and several workmen, as it was still under construction at this date. The site of Western Lodge today is taken by Sillwood Terrace, with the shops and flats above that front onto Western Road.

The next deed from 34 Sillwood Road is dated 10th April 1871 and concerns the building of the house for its first owner, Elizabeth de Lannoy. She agrees with Sir David Scott's sons, Sir James Sibbald David Scott and Montagu David Scott, to 'build and complete fit for habitation' . . two dwelling houses . . within the space of eighteen calendar months from the date hereof'. The cost of each house was not to be less than £900. The next agreement, on 23rd June of that year, was between the two Scott sons and Jabez Reynolds, the builder. He agreed to the time limit of 'eighteen calendar months from the date thereof', thus referring back to the April contract, and had to complete in a 'proper and workmanlike manner to the satisfaction of Mr. Lainson of No 170 North Street, Brighton' (mentioned in chapter 8). This was the Scott's chosen architect, but they safeguarded themselves from any falling out with him by inserting the clause 'or in case of his death or ceasing to be such Architect as aforesaid then any such other Architect as they may appoint'.

'Gothic House and Western Lodge'
Oil on paper by John Constable – inscribed '2 August 1824'.
Western Lodge was built by the Wilds father and son in about 1817. The Gothic House was built a few years later by Wilds and Busby and is their only known design in the Georgian Gothic style. Built originally as one dwelling, it was later converted into three houses (Robson and Macdonald, undated).

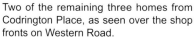

This house, and its painted neighbour to the right behind trees, replaced the bungalow mansion called Hampton Lodge, which was sold by Codrington's grandson in 1899. These existing houses were built between the 1899 sale and the new shop fronts being built in Western Road in 1903. They are similar to the c1870 semi-detached mansion blocks built on the Workhouse land around Buckingham Road and Dyke Road, opposite the old Children's Hospital.

Two of the remaining three homes from Codrington Place, as seen over the shop fronts on Western Road.

Elizabeth de Lannoy was a local philanthropist who lived in Crowborough in the late 1800s. While there is no record of her being a resident of Brighton, in the 1871 census she is renting 10 Sillwood Place, with her housemaid, cook and housekeeper, presumably to be near the building of her investments in Sillwood Road. Elizabeth is described as being 52 years old, born in Peckham, Surrey, and with 'income from annuities and shareholder of private properties'.

Her two houses, numbers 33 and 34, have identical interiors, even down to fine details of carpentry, but 34 was given a much larger garden, taking half that of number 33's. This gives the impression that Elizabeth might have planned to live at 34, but for some reason it never happened. The builder Reynolds seems to have had a contract with Lainson to build the first ten of the houses in the terrace, with Kelly's Directories indicating the last five, at the top of the road, were added by 1875. Reynolds is also mentioned in Erredge (1862) regarding a 'new street having recently been laid out to the west of the Sussex Hotel, in Cliftonville. The houses there are being built by Mr. Jabez Reynolds, of Brighton, on a large scale, and bids fair to form one of the finest streets in the parish'. He also built a number of churches for Wagner. Bearing in mind the number of schools that were operating in the Clifton/Powis area during the mid-1800s, the Scott sons were clearly not impressed by their effect on a residential street. Included in their list of 'offensive or otherwise' activities which were not allowed in Sillwood Road was 'in particular the business of School keeping'.

It was noted in chapter 7 that the whole of the Codrington Estate was sold as one unit in May 1899, so Hampton Lodge was demolished at the turn of the century and the four-storey houses were put in its place when Western Road was widened. At the same time the shops were built in the front gardens of the nine Codrington Place houses, and of the demolished Hampton Lodge. It was probably at this time that the ornate shop front was added to Sutton Lodge, on the corner of Hampton Place.

The development of Western Road as a business and commercial centre was tied up with the residential development of Church Hill and West Hill, which in turn was connected with the railway coming to town. As we have seen, the initial development of Montpelier Road was tied to the building of Kemp's Temple in 1819, and at that time it only served his house. A few years later, when it was extended northwards, it joined the main road up to the Dyke, and later became a station route from the seafront, the Brunswick Estate and the new commercial centre of Western Road, once Buckingham Place and Terminus Road had been built. But the 'new road', discussed in depth in chapter 7, which ran from the station up along Clifton Road, Powis Road and then down through Hampton Place, was a shorter distance.

The business travellers coming into the station and having the new Western Road shops as their destination had three choices of route. They could drive down Queens Road and into the congestion of the centre of town, or go north from the station up Terminus Road, skirt around the north of Church Hill encountering far less congestion, and travel down Montpelier Road. However, the third and shortest route was north from the station again, but rather than travel as far as Montpelier Road, just past the northern end of Clifton Street, they could bear left down the newly established route of Clifton Road, Powis Road, Montpelier Street and Hampton Place, right to the centre of Western Road. The route directly west from the station, up Gloucester Road, was of course too steep for horse drawn vehicles. The development of Western Road did not wait for the station to actually open, and the effects of the coming railway seemed to be well anticipated. In Leppard's 1839–1840 street directory the business advertisements tell their own story. S. Stepney, carver, gilder and picture frame maker at 25 Western Road 'has recently moved from Cranbourne Street' and J. Colby, 'Chemist and Druggist to The Queen . . . late of Castle Square, has newly moved to 34 Montpelier Road, near Christ Church'.

Traders were moving out of the small, damp premises and congested streets of the centre of town. There was no royal patronage left to keep them there, they could probably do without the seasonal custom of the new day-trippers, and the larger modern business premises along Western Road had as their geographical client base the affluent and quickly growing Clifton, Montpelier and Powis estates.

The corner of Western Road and Hampton Place.

The large white painted house is Sutton Lodge, with its later ornate addition to the front. Immediately behind Sutton Lodge is the unpainted Codrington House, and to the left of these was Fauntleroy's bungalow mansion, Hampton Lodge.

The southern end of Montpelier Road, the section south of Christ Church, was quite well established by the early 1830s. In Pigott & Co's 'National, London and Provincial Commercial Directory' a number of Montpelier Road residents are listed, but all in the lower numbers. Robert Moorcock is at number 7, the Rev. George Millett is at 9, Miss Elizabeth Bolland at 10 and Mrs. Willcock at number 13.

Hampton Villa, originally a detached house on the corner of what later became Montpelier Street and Upper North Street, pre-dates its immediate neighbours on the northern side of Montpelier Terrace by over ten years. The deeds to number 11 Montpelier Terrace date the sale of the land for that house to 1841, and the canopied villa development of this northern side of Montpelier Terrace, between Montpelier Villas and Montpelier Street, started in 1843, with Henry Faithfull's Summer House on the southern side certainly built by 1830.

In Kelly's 1845 Directory, and by the 1845 Brighton & Hove Directory, north-side Montpelier Terrace has numbers 2 to 11 noted, with John Peto's gentleman's boarding school at 4 and 5, but numbers 1, 6 and 7 are not occupied, and there is only Summer House opposite them, on the southern side. The Directories and the rate books for Montpelier Terrace are difficult to reconcile. In the 1840 Burial Rate Book numbers 1 to 10 are all occupied, with Peto's school already leasing numbers 4 and 5. But these 10 houses are not all on the northern side, because 9 is entered as Henry Faithfull's house and stable, which is known to have been on the south side. This listing of 1 to 10 in 1840 does tie in with the deeds to 11, which dated that land sale to 1841. In the 1844 Poor Rate Book the numbers for Peto's school and Faithfull's home remain the same, but numbers 6, 7 and 8 are not mentioned and in the 1845 Poor Rates, while Peto is at 3 and 4, numbers 6, 7 and 8 are listed as 'ground', Faithfull's house is numbered 14 and Capt. Martin is living at 15. All this indicates considerable movement of numbers, which is not unusual, but also that in 1843/44 there was undeveloped land on plots 6, 7 and 8, which might explain the differing architectural styles of the Terrace.

This north side of Montpelier Terrace consists of a row of seven tall flat-fronted homes from Montpelier Road in the west up to Montpelier Villas. In chapter 11 Wagner and Dale (1983) are quoted as writing that Mary Ann Wagner developed houses in Montpelier Place and Montpelier Terrace. In the Terrace these would have been the first section of numbers 1 to 5, which have a formal, if not austere, feel to them similar to some west of the junction on the south side of Montpelier Place. Numbers 6 and 7, leading to the corner of Montpelier Villas, change in style with their overhanging eaves, and seem to form a link to the different architecture of the next section of the terrace. These are six quite different Regency-style homes, numbers 8 to 13, which lead up to the turning that was becoming Montpelier Street at much the same time, and are surely not in the style of the vicar's sister. Finally there is the single Hampton Villa, built before the Terrace, and sometimes included in it, sometimes not. However, with 11's land sale dated 1841, presumably the present numbers 13 down to 9 were developed in the middle part of the 1840s, with numbers 1 to 5 at the western end a few years earlier, but the plots either side of the Montpelier Villas turning, numbers 6, 7 and 8, listed as 'ground' in 1845, were the last to be built on this northern side.

The change in style from number 6 up to the end of the canopied villas at number 13 begins to tie in with the personal recollections from J.S. Gray quoted in chapter 9. Gray recalls that in conversations with his grandfather-in-law he was told that it was the same builder who produced 6 to 13 Montpelier Terrace and all of Montpelier Villas. Since there is general agreement that A.H. Wilds was the architect of Montpelier Villas, it seems likely that he also designed these final numbers in Montpelier Terrace. With 6, 7 and 8 appearing to be the last houses built in the Terrace, the suggestion is that Wilds, with his appointed builder, erected 9 to 13 in the Terrace, then started on all 20 of Montpelier Villas together with 6, 7 and 8 in the Terrace as a single undertaking.

By Kelly's 1846 Directory there is listed all fourteen homes on this side of Montpelier Terrace, and the first two houses in Montpelier Villas are recorded as being occupied, number 1 is owned by Miss Roberts, and Thomas Birch owns number 11. It is also by this date that another home on the other side has appeared in the directories: Capt. Thomas Martin R.N., living in Montpelier Lodge, becomes the near neighbour to Henry Faithfull in Summer House. Montpellier Hall, first owned by, and presumably built for Henry Smithers, a local brewer who became the mayor of Brighton in 1861, first appears in the street directories in 1852, although in its own published history booklet the house is described as being built in 1849 to the design of A.H.Wilds. Standing between Summer House and the eastern side of Montpelier Lodge, the fourth house on the south side was Arnold House, owned by the brewer Henry Catt, and it is first named as such in the 1854 directories. However, Montpelier Lodge and Arnold House were built well before that date, but in architectural style were a little ahead of their time, and the two houses were very similar, as the next illustration shows. Only the Lodge remains today, and with its projecting eaves and supporting brackets, and the gently arched window lintels, it is very much in the early Victorian – post 1840 – tradition. But in modern legal correspondence relating to this house, reference is made to a covenant dated 25th March 1830. The covenant is between John Moore and William Borrer (the Sussex botanist) and places considerable restrictions on what could be built in the gardens of Montpelier Lodge, adding that if any small garden outbuildings were erected, they must not obstruct the view south or south-west from Henry Faithfull's Summer House. Dating this south side of Montpelier Terrace is difficult, hampered in part by the complete lack of any eighteenth or nineteenth century engravings of the area and partly by rather vague street directories. On the 1824/25 Pigott-Smith map at the end of this chapter, it is assumed that the two semi-detached homes on this site are Montpelier Lodge and Arnold House. If they are not, then the only possibility is that between the map of 1825, and the covenant of 1830, the two houses on the map were demolished and replaced by the Lodge and Arnold House. This is quite a likely explanation, and would give the logical assumption that Faithfull's 1830 restrictive deed was in response to the two replacement houses being built at that date. They would have been built on Faithfull's land, either leased or sold by him, but with covenants dictating what could be built beside his own Summer House.

At the southern end of Hampton Place, on the northern side of the exit-way from Waitrose car park, there can still be seen small outbuildings today, and these are the remains of the stable blocks that were certainly used by Montpelier Lodge, probably by Summer House as well, and later by Montpellier Hall. Returning to Mr. Catt's ownership of Montpelier Lodge, by the mid 1860s Catt had come into a considerable fortune and changed his name to Henry Willett, as a requirement of the inheritance. His wife was Frances Jane and he owned the West Street Brewery. There was a daughter, Florence Marion, and two sons, Edgar William who was a London surgeon, then Percy Arnold who was in the brewing business. Willett died on 24th February 1905 and left £233,824. 2. 10p in his estate.

Arnold House as an hotel in the early twentieth century. Initially the house was flat-fronted, before the front porch and balcony addition built on by the hotel owner. Imagining this house without the added porch and the later squared bay-window on the left, it is much the same as the present day Montpelier Lodge.

Henry Faithfull died on the 17th February 1851, aged 56, and his widow, Margaret, originally from Ross-on-Wye, seems to have immediately sold Summer House to Samuel Matthews, and then she died a year later in Wivelsfield. By the 1854 Town Rate Book (ESRO BH/B/4/37/2) the Faithfull home was owned by Price Bowen. The back gardens of these four villas on this south side of Montpelier Terrace extended down the slope and abutted Codrington Place, with its terrace of nine homes whose front gardens extended further down the hill to form the northern side of Western Road. With the demand for terraces all around them, it is interesting how these four large villas on the south side of Montpelier Terrace remained so select. As mentioned on the previous page, the possibility is that when Henry Faithfull the solicitor bought the land for his own new home from Kemp, he established covenants whereby he retained control of what his future neighbours could build. This idea is strengthened, first, by the fact that the land for the building of Montpellier Hall was purchased from Faithfull, and secondly by the aforementioned March 1830 covenant applied to the Lodge. Only the Hall and Montpelier Lodge are still standing today.

The early nineteenth century development in the West Laine, particularly along Cliff Butts, where Regency Square is today, and further west to include the coastal end of Montpelier Road and stretching inland from there, produced some impressive villas, and by the 1814 rates revaluation they were among the most valuable homes in the town (Berry 2005). But the end of the early Georgian period saw rising land values, and then with the coming of the Regency and early Victorian developments, most of these villas were either demolished or included in later terraces built around them – such was the Prince Regent's influence on architectural design, the use of new building materials, and the general excitement among the builders and architects of the period to produce these new style houses. In our area the clearest illustration of this change of architectural sentiment is between the first tall, flat-fronted section of north-side Montpelier Terrace and the second section of smaller canopied homes with the deep, bracketed, projecting eaves. Both were built during the 1840s, but they represent two distinct building styles for town-centre homes. However it appears that if Montpelier Lodge and Arnold House were the original homes on this site, they escaped this early Victorian demolition. These two houses can be seen on J. Pigott Smith's 'Map of the Town of Brighton and its environs – delineated from Actual Surveys made in the year 1824/5' (illustrated later in the chapter). They had large gardens that stretched down the slope towards Lady Gosford's home, West Hill Lodge, and Hampton Lodge, both on Western Road. In Pigott Smith's map they are drawn as attached houses which was obviously not the case, although the space between them was in-filled with extra rooms later.

Upper North Street developed in the usual fashion, with buildings going up in no particular order. By 1846 there were 25 listed occupants, mostly traders, but ranging in house number from 4 up to 109, so many of the undeveloped plots were assigned a number. However, as usual these changed, so John Pointer, the landlord of the Windmill Inn, was number 54 in 1846, but number 63 two years later.

Hampton Villa was owned by Richard Lane by 1846, and by this date John Bradshaw had moved his business to 55 King's Road. Lane was one of the proprietors of Brighton College, and by the census record of 1851 the house was occupied by a 67-year-old wine merchant, John Haffenden, with his wife Ann, two sons and two servants (Doyne-Ditmas 2000). In 1864 it began a long lease to St. Mary Magdalen Church across the road. The church itself was built in 1861 on the site of a timber yard, and its first vicar was an Anglican convert from Hove, the Rev. George Oldham, described as a 'Missionary Rector'. He died in Hampton Villa on 18th October 1875, aged 55. Further clergy lived in the house until 1885, and by about 1890 the present presbytery was built next to the church. The timber yard on which the church was built was presumably the source of much of the local woodwork for the new houses in the area. Up the western side of Hampton Villa, a start was made on Montpelier Street during the latter part of 1845, and by the next year four houses are occupied: numbers 1, 2, 3 and 6. The carpenter Richard Trower lived at number 6, no doubt another of the craftsmen working on houses in the area.

A little to the east a start had been made on Victoria Street during 1840, with numbers 1,6,7,8,23,27 and 37 listed in the rate book of that year (BH/B/4/34/1). Francis Hallett was the landlord, and presumably he and his son were the builders, of numbers 6 and 7, while number 1 is noted as 'a new house'. That notation in the 1840 rate book rather implies that there were no other 'new houses' under construction at that particular time. Joy Moore (undated) refers to Victoria Street's entry in the 1841 census, where she notes that the houses were not numbered, although they were according to the rate book of the previous year. By the 1846 Directory number 30 was occupied by a builder, and at number 12 lived Thomas Willmot, carpenter, builder and undertaker. Between them, the rate books and the Directories suggest that Victoria Street took some time to develop, and by the 1850 Directory only 14 of the 37 available plots are numbered and occupied. It is not until the 1854 rate book that the numbers go up to 45. Regarding the spelling of Montpelier, in all the hand-written rate books up to 1854 it is spelt with two 'l's, as it is in most of the Directories in the 1840s. But by the Directories from 1850 it usually has only one.

Bearing in mind that Church Hill – West Side was very much an area of craftsmen and tradesmen, the odd development of these streets, with a house or two here, another there, is because individual builders and carpenters purchased and worked on just one or two plots at a time, sometimes living in the house as soon as they could, and then developed other houses in the street, with bricklayer, builder and carpenter working together and generally living on site whenever their first house was habitable. And the Hallett family's original 1835 lease agreement on much of this land from Kemp would have meant that many of these builders and craftsmen were either working for the Halletts or were buying plots from them. Thus G.W. Sawyer was involved with the building of Clifton Terrace in 1846, and a few years later he is working from Victoria House, with partners, almost certainly on the houses in Victoria and Montpelier Streets. Similarly Thomas Wisden, builder and brickmaker, is living at 15 Hampton Place in 1845, and Joseph Wisden (builder) is the owner/occupier of 8 Victoria Street in 1844. By 1849 Thomas Wisden is involved in land purchases to build 3 and 4 Clifton Hill, and other houses further up the northern side of the Hill, having most probably been the builder of the detached houses in Clifton Road a couple of years earlier.

The deeds to 1 Hampton Terrace, next door to Hampton Villa, indicate the dealings over this part of West Hill between Kemp and Francis Hallett, detailing the lease between these two gentlemen dated 8th December 1835 (this document is mentioned in chapter 3 as part of the Victoria House history). The house deeds are dated 18th September 1848 and make reference to this indenture of December 1835 and to another agreement dated 29/30th December 1837 involving William Hallett, Henry Faithfull and George Molyneux. William Hallett, in conjunction with his father Francis, obviously had partners in his land purchases and development of this part of West Hill, rather as Yearsley did later. So on 18th September 1848 William Hallett sold the land for 1 Hampton Terrace to Joseph Vine for £100, and the deeds record that a house had been built on the plot. A second deed dated the following day details a mortgage to Joseph Vine for £300 from an artist, Edward Fox. Thus when Hallett sold the land to Vine, the house had been built. As in the Powis area, land sale and house sale were frequently dealt with as separate transactions. The price also reflects the terms of the Kemp/Francis Hallett lease agreement. Land and house came to £400, and in chapter 3 it is noted that £400 is the minimum value under the terms of the lease. Since William Hallett was the owner, developer and builder, it seems clear that he built 1 Hampton Terrace, which reinforces the belief that he also built Hampton Villa next door some 16 years earlier.

A further deed attached to 1 Hampton Terrace informs us that Vine did not stay long in the house. There is a 'grant of equity' dated 2nd January 1849 where Henry Burgess, a butcher, took over the mortgage from Vine, eventually paying it off to Fox in the sum of £300 plus interest on 18th November 1871. Burgess is then recorded as having title to the house and land. One of the detailed descriptions in the 1848 deed is of the original dwarf wall with railings, which can still be seen in the front of the four Hampton Terrace houses. An earlier address for 1 Hampton Terrace was 58 Upper North Street, but the address for these four terrace houses must have taken its name from Hampton Villa at a fairly early date. The name 'Hampton Terrace' nearly appeared as A.H. Wilds' grand plans for the north side of Western Road some 23 years earlier – Wilds' engraving of the plan is illustrated in the next chapter. Looking again at the Hallett's 99-year lease agreement with Kemp in 1835, it is very likely that at some stage Hallett had managed to convert this to freehold purchase, either with Kemp or with his widow.

Moving towards the sea, Sir David Scott (1782–1851) had a home in Brighton by 1818, and purchased the unfinished Oriental Place development in 1827. He employed A.H. Wilds to complete it for him, and build his new home in the town, Sillwood House. Sir David had inherited the Baronetcy and Silwood Park, Berkshire. Oriental Place is immediately south of Sillwood Street, and Scott's country home is obviously the origin of the name, although it took until 1870 for Western Cottages to be re-named Sillwood Road.

Detail of the 'Panorama of Brighton', drawn by A.H.Wilds and engraved in aquatint by A. Edington. Published by W.H. Mason, Brighton, and Ackermann & Co., London, 1833.

In the above illustration the street coming down to the seafront, just left of centre, is the southern end of Montpelier Road. The central building is West Cliffe House, listed in the 1846 Post Office Directory as a lodging house owned by William Beck. To the right, in the distance, at the top of Oriental Place, is Sir David Scott's Sillwood House. This engraving represents the only known image of Sillwood House, as the other panorama of the seafront, by Robert Havell, was published in 1824, a few years too early. This is also the clearest view of Montpelier Road as it joins King's Road.

Again the earlier Havell scene, entitled 'A Coasting View of Brighton', shows West Cliffe House with the junction beside it, but because the artist depicts the seafront from many yards out to sea, the scale is too small to be clearly discerned.

The incomplete Oriental Place and Gardens development that Scott took over was the brainchild of the botanist Henry Phillips (note 8). The proposed large domed construction, to be called the Athenaeum, immediately north of the present Oriental Place, was to house rare botanical specimens, cover an acre of land (Ford 1981) and be overlooked from the north by the grand Hampton Terrace which was planned for the north side of Western Road (illustrated next chapter). In the end the building work that Scott actually developed, apart from his own new house, were the homes either side of Oriental Place, together with the eastern side of the terrace on the seafront, seen far right in the 'Panorama of Brighton' print above.

The Wilds print of the proposed Oriental Place development (illustrated below) was published c1825. Comparing the left hand side of this print of 1825 with the 'Panorama of Brighton' print of 1833, raises difficulties with the southern end of Montpelier Road, as it entered the King's Road. The western side of the sea front terrace that Wilds proposed covered the land on which this

'Perspective View of Oriental Place, West Cliff, Brighton,
leading to the Athenaeum and Oriental Garden'
Aquatint engraving by George Hunt after A.H. Wilds, published by
C. & R. Sickelmore, Brighton c.1825.
The left hand section of this terrace, had it been built, would have blocked the southern end of Montpelier Road. From the gap in the building line it looks as if Wilds was suggesting that Montpelier Road should turn east and enter Oriental Place just behind this front terrace.

end of Montpelier Road now stands. However, according to the Pigott-Smith map of 1824/25 the junction of Montpelier Road with the sea front was already in place. In the 'Panorama of Brighton' print, West Cliff House stands between Montpelier Road and the turning into Oriental Place, and it is a relatively small building with just three bays to it. In the print opposite, Wilds is suggesting that the much larger left hand terrace facing us should stand on that piece of ground. As the following Pigott-Smith map already has Montpelier Road in that position, presumably Wilds had in mind that Montpelier Road's southerly route should end behind his new terrace, then turn either left or right and go around it to reach the King's Road.

In the end this area could be viewed as one of broken architectural dreams. The grand schemes that were never built include the large Hampton Terrace to the north, the Athenaeum with the library, museum and reading room, and one side of the large seafront terraces of Oriental Place. How different the southern boundaries of the Montpelier district might have looked – on a par with Brunswick if all had been built as planned.

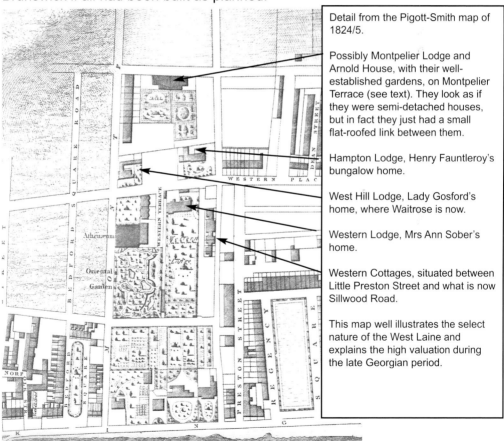

Detail from the Pigott-Smith map of 1824/5.

Possibly Montpelier Lodge and Arnold House, with their well-established gardens, on Montpelier Terrace (see text). They look as if they were semi-detached houses, but in fact they just had a small flat-roofed link between them.

Hampton Lodge, Henry Fauntleroy's bungalow home.

West Hill Lodge, Lady Gosford's home, where Waitrose is now.

Western Lodge, Mrs Ann Sober's home.

Western Cottages, situated between Little Preston Street and what is now Sillwood Road.

This map well illustrates the select nature of the West Laine and explains the high valuation during the late Georgian period.

11

The Prints of the Area and Some Early Houses

Apart from the usual areas of research into the history of any town, the Brighton historian's work is greatly facilitated by the many eighteenth and nineteenth century artists, engravers and lithographers who illustrated the town (note 9). Between them, these artists and craftsmen produced more pre-photographic views of Brighton than have been made of any other town or city in the United Kingdom, outside the capital. There were over 1,300 Georgian, Regency and Victorian engravings and lithographs of Brighton town itself published by the early 1860s, and this figure does not include some of the small steel plates and lithographs included in the many guides and tourist booklets that were published every year, or the wood engravings in the magazine/newspaper publications of the late 1800s. The other aspect of fortune for which we can be thankful was the advent of the steel engraving. By the 1820s some of the important London print publishers like Rudolph Ackermann were changing from copper to steel plates for a limited number of their publications. So by the 1840s and '50s Brighton publishers such as Grant, Wilmott or Leppard were freely using this new medium to produce small scenes with high quality detail and in greater numbers, all qualities which were impossible with the softer copper. With the arrival of the railway visitors these smaller, sometimes almost 'tourist illustration' prints, had a wider market than the relatively rich and limited clientele of the Georgian print publisher, so this increased production has greatly benefited the 21st century Brighton print collector. The only unfortunate aspectof this print publishers' success story was that the Clifton/Montpelier/ Powis area is a little lacking in this artistic representation, for reasons explained earlier in the text.

In their book *Images of Brighton* (1981), John and Jill Ford brought together all the known views of Brighton up to the early 1860s, and many views in and around our area can be found therein. On the eastern boundary of our area there are some forty engravings of St. Nicholas' Church, and glimpses of the Clifton landscape can be seen in the backgrounds of some of these. On the far western boundary there are seven known views of Kemp's home, the

Temple in Montpelier Road. In addition to these two specific subjects, there are 21 other nineteenth century engravings relevant to Church Hill. Most are illustrated here, and the details of a few are worth highlighting. In Richard Nibbs' 'View of Brighton from Hudson's Mill' (chapter 2) there is depicted the only view of the grounds of the Church Hill Workhouse; in the 1866 view of St. Michael and All Angels' Church (chapter 3) can be seen a unique view of some of the homes on the north side of Victoria Road, and an engraving of Christ Church (chapter 3) illustrates the only view of some of the tall terraces at the southern end of Montpelier Road. Mrs. Watts' advertisement of 1839 (chapter 8) illustrates the first house built in Clifton Hill, before it was so named, and one of the Montpelier Crescent engravings (chapter 8) gives us a glimpse of Mr. Yearsley's first house in Clifton Hill, probably in the year it was built, 1845. The view of the proposed Hampton Terrace, c1825, (this chapter) shows us West Hill Lodge on the corner of Montpelier Road and Western Road, the present site of Waitrose, together with Hampton Lodge near the corner of Western Road and Hampton Place. The most complete view we have of the developed area is the J. Newman c1850 lithograph of the 'West View of Brighton from the top of The Old Church' (chapter 2). This print shows Dyke Road at the junction of Church Street, then Norman Lodge and most of Clifton Terrace. The houses being built down Clifton Place are in the distance, as is part of Upper North Street and the spire of Christ Church in Montpelier Road. Having just 21 prints in and around our area, aside from the Church and the Temple, needs to be seen in context. For example, there are 14 prints each of the Victoria Fountain and of Brighton Station, and 45 views of the Steine. Bearing in mind that the Clifton/Powis/Montpelier estate represents the earliest and most important Victorian development in Brighton, the claim that this area missed out on Brighton's print-making heritage seems justified.

Returning to the prints of Kemp's Temple home, it is one of these that is of great interest to this study, number 1042 in Fords' *Images of Brighton*. This print is from William Daniell's series *A Voyage Round Great Britain* and is a coloured aquatint published in 1823 entitled 'Ovington near Brighton', which is a complete misnomer for this print (illustrated page 157).

This series by Daniell filled eight volumes with approximately 318 hand coloured copper-plate engravings, and with that weight of work in a publication of this period there will always be mistakes. In another Brighton print from this publication Daniell recorded the title as 'Near Regent's Square' when the location's correct name was of course 'Regency Square'. Daniell also recorded the Temple as being designed by Nash, whereas it was most likely the Wilds father and son team, as described by Mr. Robins in his 1844 auction description. The house was said to have been built according to the dimensions of Solomon's Temple, found in chapter 6 of the First Book of Kings.

If this was the case it might say something of Kemp's modesty, for he surely knew that in chapter 7 Solomon's personal house was twice the size of the Jewish Temple that he built.

In this engraving of 'Ovington near Brighton' we are viewing the Temple from its eastern side, the sea is on the left and we are on a road at the brow of a hill that is descending away from us and a little to our right. With such an arrangement of the terrain, and that view of the Temple, the artist is clearly standing on the present Children's Hospital site. The road in the foreground, which six people are walking along, is Kemp's 'Road to Blatchington', the present Clifton Hill (which track is clearly defined on an 1822 map of Brighton). The corn field between the artist and the Temple, farmed by William Acton according to the hospital deeds, makes up precisely that area of land mentioned in Thomas Read Kemp's will and purchased by John Yearsley, as seen before a house had been built on it. Brighton Art Gallery has a Daniell pencil sketch of the Ovington print, purchased by them in 1997. The notes say that Daniell's tour round the country lasted 12 years, and adds that it is known the artist arrived in Sussex in 1823.

The Catalogue entry in John and Jill Ford's *Images of Brighton* reads, 'The title of this view of The Temple is mysterious. . .' and in the text they make the point that Daniell had obviously confused the house with that of Nathaniel Kemp's at Ovingdean, so its incorrect name may have a simple explanation. When in the area, Daniell stayed with Thomas Read's uncle and trustee, Nathaniel Kemp, who lived at Ovingdean Hall, midway between Brighton and Rottingdean to the east. The Temple is towards the west of central Brighton. But with so many sketches being prepared, the artist may understandably have made the wrong association with the image. He incorrectly noted on the original drawing that it was the home of 'N. Kemp' rather than 'T. Kemp', and then probably recalled the name as being the 'Oving' part of Ovingdean, and the 'ton' part of Brighton, so arriving at the strange name of Ovington. Whether or not this is the correct reason for Daniell's mistake does not detract from the fact that this is the only nineteenth century engraving of the road that became Clifton Hill. With the artist standing on the highest point in the area, this 1823 view covers much of the land that was to become the Clifton, Montpelier and Powis estates. The only house to be seen is Kemp's Temple, on the western boundary of the area. The couple walking away from us on the left could be the young Mr. & Mrs. Kemp, with a butler in attendance behind them. To the left of the artist's position, near the eastern boundary, would have been Vine's Mill, Vine's own house further back and the mill workers' cottages, all just out of view. In the left foreground of the engraving there is a simple rustic fence, and in the painting of Vine's Mill in chapter 4 that same fence can be seen. And of course, as Daniell sat down with his sketch pad to depict this scene, the newly built Workhouse was just behind him. Today the entrance to the Temple building is facing us, on its eastern side. For Kemp the entrance was on the northern side, where there is the largest area of courtyard and the stable block. As Kemp came out of his front entrance, immediately to his left was the plantation of firs that surrounded the chalybeate spring.

'Ovington near Brighton'
Drawn, engraved in aquatint and published by William Daniell, 1823.
According to the 1822 map, illustrated in chapter 1, the first use of this route was for carriages to get to the spring, where the road ended. By the Pigott-Smith map of 1824/25 a narrow continuation of this road is depicted, taking it past the spring and on in the direction of Blatchington.

From the eastern windows of their home the Kemps would have had a good view of Vine's Mill, and of the new Workhouse just beyond. Kemp had sold Herstmonceux Place in 1819 and moved into his new home on Montpelier Road. The Workhouse was built in 1822, and the deeds to 16 Clifton Hill (ESRO AMS 6382) confirm that Kemp was the owner of the land and so must have approved of it being built within view of the Temple. When Erredge (1862) quotes the building costs he does not mention land purchase, so it had been assumed that Kemp donated the land to the church commissioners, and this would certainly have been in line with his religious convictions, and his financial security, at that time. As mentioned, Martin (1871) puts a figure of £1,600 on the land purchase, but this seems very unlikely. In chapter 1 it is established that Kemp re-purchased the whole of Church Hill from the Sackvilles for £1,610 in 1817, so it is improbable that the church commissioners would have paid a similar sum for just a small part of the land five years later.

Of the seven known engravings of the Temple, this earliest print of 1823 shows the house before the top floor was extended and before the addition of the four distinctive chimneys, which do appear in the other images of circa 1827–35. These chimneys, and the dome in their midst, were demolished in 1911–12 and replaced with dormer windows, but they raise the interesting possibility of architectural links with the Pavilion. In the 1817/1818 prints of Henry Holland's original Pavilion, probably the most distinctive feature is its shallow central dome (but no tall chimney-like minarets), and it is the next year that Kemp starts building the Temple, with one shallow central dome but no chimneys. During 1822–23, when Daniell would have drawn the Temple in its original form, Nash's rebuilding of the Pavilion was still going on. But by the prints of 1824–25, the more or less finished Pavilion had several distinctive features of a dome, albeit onion-shaped by now, surrounded by four high chimney-like minarets. And by 1827 a print of the Temple in Sickelmore's *Select Views of Brighton* shows its dome also flanked by four high chimneys (see the illustration in chapter 6 and later in this chapter).

Bearing in mind that Kemp moved into 22 Sussex Square in 1827, presumably he commissioned this dramatic change to the outline image of his house before that date – in other words, shortly after the high chimney image appeared on the Pavilion. This is something of an architectural coincidence, bearing in mind that a dome of any kind flanked by four high chimneys was not a feature of any other building in the south of England. Dale (1967) also notes the similarity – 'a large square mansion surmounted by an enormous dome, somewhat in the style of the Pavilion'. To be fair to Kemp he was not the only one to copy Henry Holland's ideas as displayed in the early Pavilion. Holland's 1787 watercolour of the Pavilion's east front shows a dome supported by the semicircle of tall columns, and a very close version of that image appears in C.A. Busby's 'Series of Designs for Villas and Country Houses', published in 1808.

This change at the Temple did have practical reasons. The original design seemed to have just one chimney in the centre of the dome – smoke appears from it in the print in chapter 7. By about 1827 the top floor, which was set back from the main building line, was extended in an east/west direction (turning this top floor into an 'H' shape, with the dome in the middle). But to join these four new rooms onto the main central chimney would have been difficult, hence each new room was given its own chimney. The best image to explain the 'H' formation of this extension is an 1845 lithograph, illustrated number 1046 in John & Jill Ford's book, while number 1043 in that book, the aforementioned Sickelmore print, best illustrates the dramatic change in outline image that the four new chimneys produced. During 1827/28 the Temple was let to a banker named Dorrien, then it was let to the Rev. Robert Fennell in late 1828 at an annual rent of £300, becoming a young gentlemen's academy (Note 10). It remained an academy until it was taken over by the Girls' Public Day School Trust in 1880.

Remembering that Daniell painted Sezincote House in Gloucestershire and Kemp's Temple, together with several other views in Brighton, it might be surprising to realize that he never painted the Royal Pavilion, albeit that it was being rebuilt during Daniell's first visit. However, the explanation is in the text of his *Voyage Round Great Britain*, where the artist writes of the Pavilion that 'there is not one feature, great or small, which at all accords with the purity, grandeur and magnificence that characterises the genuine oriental style'. A style that he thought was in ample evidence at Sezincote, being swayed possibly by the fact that his uncle, Thomas Daniell, had designed some of the smaller buildings in the grounds. The two Daniells had of course toured India in the 1780s and '90s, and the design for Sezincote followed some of their drawings. William Daniell's opinion of the Brighton building seems to be echoed by J.M.W. Turner. While Turner put nothing in writing, on his visits to Brighton in 1824 and 1828 he more or less ignored the Pavilion, making just three small 'perfunctory outlines' during his second visit, that were never enlarged upon, (Beevers 1995). Constable never recorded the building either, and while he was not an architectural artist, he did take some interest in Brighton buildings, painting 'The Gothic House and Western Lodge' and a number of local windmills. By the date of the King's final visit to Brighton in 1827, the artists' opinions seemed to be in line with some contemporary thought, that the Pavilion was 'at best a folly in doubtful taste', (Dale 1972). However, while Sezincote held the central position of the very limited Indian movement in English architecture at the beginning of the nineteenth century, in fact the Prince of Wales's Indian Stables at Brighton are thought to have been started at least two years before Sezincote took on its Indian appearance in 1805, and parts of the Gloucestershire house bear close resemblance to the stables, which was the first building in the Indian manner in this country. Maybe we should be thankful for Daniell's dislike of the Pavilion, had he spent time painting it, we might not have his early view of Clifton Hill and the Powis land.

If, in say 1838, we took an imaginary walk up Montpelier Road, the western boundary of our area, from the Montpelier Terrace junction, we would have passed three large houses on the left hand side. The first was Belvedere, a house built about 1837 for Mary Ann, the sister of the vicar of Brighton, the Rev. Henry Michell Wagner. Mary Ann never lived there, and the following illustration shows it as a girls' school, before Mary Ann died in 1868, and left the house to her brother's eldest son, the Rev. Arthur Douglas Wagner. He lived in Belvedere until his death in 1902. Wagner & Dale (1983) describe Arthur as living a very simple life at the house, his only luxuries being books and manuscripts. At his death his library comprised some 12,000 volumes, the auction sale of which took three days. The house then became the Park Royal Hotel, and was demolished c1965 when flats were built on the site.

Belvedere is a descriptive name, meaning some form of turret rising up from the roof of the house and affording fine views. In the print below the large house in the middle distance to the right could be Western House, and the church spire just in the picture far right is Christ Church, further down Montpelier Road. Apart from Belvedere, Mary Ann Wagner developed the houses that now form part of Belvedere Terrace and part of Montpelier Place and Montpelier Terrace, on three acres of land that she owned (Wagner & Dale 1983).

'Belvedere, Montpelier Road.'
As seen from the back gardens. Aquatint engraving after G.Earp, jnr., published by W.H.Mason c.1850.

The next house was the Vicarage, illustrated on the opposite page. This was home to the Wagners, and set further back from the road than was Belvedere. It was built by George Cheesman & Son in 1834/35, in the Tudor Gothic style. Erredge (1862) records that it stood in two acres of gardens.

In Wallis's 1836 guide the house is described as 'a splendid mansion near the Temple, built by a merchant of the town. The garden in front is very tastefully laid out, and the situation very ariy'.

Lithograph c.1840. The only known engraved image of the Vicarage.

The Vicarage in 2006 as part of the Brighton & Hove High School.
In 1840 the vicar paid a poor rate of £3 4s 9d a year on the house.

In the chapter on the churches of the area the similarity between George Cheesman's design for Christ Church in Montpelier Road, and that of Barry's for St. Peter's was noted. The Vicarage is another example of Cheesman's inspiration coming from established architects of the period. The following lithograph is the design of the London architect H.E. Kendall for a 'Parsonage House near Brighton'. Its exact location, or indeed if it was ever built, is not known, but the design was published by Kendall in the early 1830s, just before Cheesman started Wagner's new home, and the similarities are too remarkable for co-incidence.

Kendall's design was double fronted, not triple fronted, but apart from this detail the duplication of design with Wagner's vicarage extends to the square bay windows, the deep right-angled pediments above with the step down at each side, the tall windows with much the same depth ground floor and first floor, the small upright rectangular windows between the bays, and the tall chimneys. The only deviation Cheesman put in was to move the front door to the side. Kendall did work in Brighton, building two houses for the Marquess of Bristol in Sussex Square. He also built 24 Belgrave Square in London for Kemp. It is interesting to conjecture what he would have thought of the Rev. Wagner's new Vicarage.

'Parsonage House near Brighton'
Lithograph published by H.E.Kendall, Architect 33 Brunswick Square, London c1834.
This print shows the similarities with Wagner's Vicarage in Brighton.

The last house, having crossed the then unnamed track that led into the Wick Estate, was the Temple, home to Mr. & the 2nd Mrs. Thomas Read Kemp until 1827, and the first of our three 'Montpelier Road Houses' to have been built.

'The Temple, seat of T.R.Kemp Esqr', showing the four high chimneys now surrounding its central dome and the 'H' formation of the new top floor.

This 'unnamed track' to Wick is now Temple Gardens, but in Folthorpe's 1848 Directory it is listed as 'Furse Hill Road – turning out of the Montpelier Road between the Vicarage and Temple House School'. It led to the then recently built Windlesham House, now flats but previously the New Sussex Hospital for Women. Windlesham House has an interesting history connected to the remarkable Mrs. Louisa Martindale, who helped start the Brighton branch of the Women Suffrage Society. In 1906 she had set up a dispensary for women and children in Brighton, which was eventually converted to a hospital for women, in answer to the many pleas from her patients to be seen by a lady doctor. There was enormous opposition to her work, but in 1918, four years after Louisa died, one of her daughters, Dr. Louisa Martindale, purchased Windlesham House and it became known as the New Sussex Hospital for Women. Windlesham played an important medical part in the women's movement in Sussex, and one of Dr. Martindale's supporters who helped raise the funds to buy the house was Dr. Octavia Wilberforce, the great granddaughter of William. In about 1924, after working in London hospitals, Octavia purchased 24 Montpelier Crescent and began her general practice from there, as well as working in the New Women's Hospital. Number 24 then became the district office for the Red Cross in Brighton, and it is now a doctor's surgery once again.

Windlesham House itself started life as Windlesham School for boys, built by the headmaster, Lt. Charles Robert Maldon, in 1844. It was named after his wife's favourite village in Surrey, just east of Bagshot, and as the local roads were built, they were named after the house. Maldon had moved his pupils out of the house in the November of 1913 and his mother, who owned the building, put the house up for sale for £4,000, asking an additional £6,000 for the extensive grounds. It being such a difficult time nationally, the house did not sell, but by the early summer of 1918 Dr. Martindale and her trustees decided to purchase it for their hospital plans. Then in June of that year Canon Dormer Pierce put the Vicarage up for sale at £8,000. This was seen as a far more suitable building for a hospital, so subject to the priest finding suitable alternative accommodation, Martindale's trustees agreed to buy it rather than Windlesham. Unfortunately they had not anticipated such an awkward priest who was unable to find another house that quite suited his taste. After many difficult meetings, even with the Bishop, interest in the Vicarage was abandoned and the Windlesham School House became the new hospital. The Vicarage was finally taken over by the Girls' Public Day School Trust in December 1922 (Brown 2006), but how easily the history of these two houses could have been swapped.

By the time of our imaginary 1838 walk the Temple had been the Rev. Robert Fennell's academy for ten years, and we have passed three grand houses – Belvedere, the Vicarage and the Temple – with the two closely linked families of Kemp and Wagner. Moving to Montpelier Road from Hertsmonceux, and after nearly twenty years of isolation, Kemp's first immediate neighbour was the vicar of Brighton, the Rev. Henry Michell Wagner (1792–1870), whose brother, George Henry Malcolm Wagner (1786-1868), had later lived at Herstmonceux Place, leasing it from the trustees of W.D. Gillon, MP for Falkirk, to whom Kemp had sold it. George Henry's second son was also baptised at Herstmonceux. The Rev. Henry Michell Wagner's father was not in the church, but had made his fortune as a hatter to George II, and had married Anne Elizabeth, daughter of the Rev. Henry Michell, a previous Vicar of Brighton who died in 1789. It was this family money that enabled the Rev. Henry Wagner and his son, the Rev. Arthur Douglas Wagner, to be so influential and generous in the building of churches in Brighton.

The Wick Estate to the west, the grounds of which included the chalybeate spring, was bought from the Rev. Thomas Scutt by Kemp in 1825, but with his problems in Kemp Town he was forced to sell it to Sir Isaac Lyon Goldsmid in 1830. Goldsmid then commissioned the architect Decimus Burton to build a new home initially called Furze Hill, but quickly re-named Wick Hall. Burton was a London architect who had already designed the Colosseum in Regent's Park and the Athenaeum in Pall Mall. In 1830 he published an ambitious plan for a proposed rustic village of detached villas at Furze Hill. In the end Wick Hall was the only residence to be built. There is some confusion over Wick Hall and Wick House, the two names often being interchanged as if they are referring to the same house. In fact Wick House, on the Rev. Scutt's original estate, is the earlier one, and in Wallis (1836) is described as being, from 1829, the residence of the Rev. Dr. Everard who, in conjunction with the Rev. Wagner, was charged with issuing admission tickets to the Chapel Royal. On the eastern side of the Wick Estate, Wick Hall was Goldsmid's house, built once he had bought the estate after Kemp defaulted on the original purchase agreement with Scutt. Both are clearly shown on a map in Robertson's Brighton & Hove booklet, c1899. Wick Hall, quoted as being 'one of Burton's finest villas' (Middleton 1979), was demolished in 1935. Wick House was pulled down just before the outbreak of the second world war and Furze Croft flats now stand on its site. 'Furze' is an early English name for land covered in gorse.

By the early 1850s Montpelier Road had many more dwellings, in the form of the large terraces that we see today. Turning off King's Road at number 142, Folthorp's 1856 Directory gives Montpelier Road numbers 1 – 65 and, as noted, the architecture of the north-west corner of Montpelier Road and Place is of the Brunswick Square and Powis Square design. Next came Belvedere House, followed by the Vicarage, then the Rev. W.H.Gutteridge in Temple House School, then numbers 70–99, followed by Clayton House and Silwood House. These were all on the west side.

By the late 1840s and early '50s Montpelier Road was fast becoming a version of London's Harley Street. There were the physicians William King at 23, next door to Christ Church, and Dr. William Kebbell living at number 29. Also in the road, and described as principal surgeons, were William Shoveller at number 4, Mr. W. Whitehouse at 35 (George Browne had taken over his practice by 1856), Mr. T.B. Winter at number 28, W.W. Stafford at 64, J. Steel at 82 and G.F.Hodgson at 91. Other surgeons living in the area at this date were Charles Brown at 13 Montpelier Terrace, Benjamin Guinness and John Terry, both in Montpelier Street and Henry Sutton at 61 Upper North Street. Thomas Andrews had lived at 12 Montpelier Road in the mid 1840s. By the late 1860s, when Denmark Terrace became established, it too carried on this medical tradition, with the surgeon C. Willett at number 2, R. Massey MD at number 17 and Alfred George Field, surgeon, at 22. The medical profession in Brighton may have been attracted to Montpelier Road by its association with the French spa town, through its proximity to our own spa waters in St. Ann's Well Gardens – possibly in order to outdo the health giving qualities of anywhere else in Europe. An interesting quote is given in Andrews and Crisfield (2006). They refer to a treatise of 1843 by Dr. Arthur Wigan, who claims that 'many invalids . . . have recovered immediately when sent to the top of Montpelier Road . . .'

Towards the southern end of Montpelier Road, contemporary with the Temple but built before the other two grand houses mentioned, was West Hill Lodge, the home of the Countess Dowager of Gosford. As noted, this house stood on the present site of Waitrose supermarket, on the corner of Western Road and Montpelier Road, and was still there on the map of 1875. The following illustration of Hampton Terrace illustrates the grand but unfulfilled plans for these lower slopes of the hill, and shows how easily the dominant name of the area might have been Hampton rather than Montpelier.

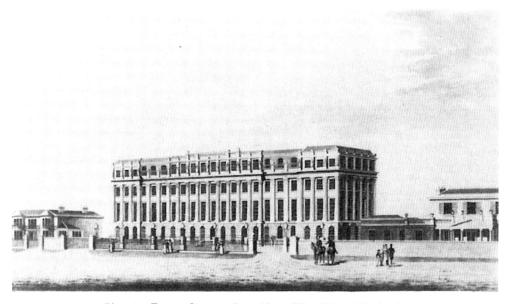

'Hampton Terrace Commanding a View of The Oriental Gardens'.
Aquatint engraving by George Hunt after A.H. Wilds, c 1825.

Published c.1825, this was Wilds' proposed development on the north side of what is now Western Road, between Montpelier Road and Hampton Place. West Hill Lodge is far left and Hampton Lodge, not very faithfully depicted, is on the far right. In the end nothing was built until the nine terraced homes of Codrington Place by 1846. The gardens to the Codrington Place houses were on precisely this piece of land for which the above Hampton Terrace was proposed. Where figures walk and ride on horseback in the picture is now Western Road, and the artist is standing on the later site of the present Sillwood Road, then called Western Cottages. Behind and to the left of the artist was Mrs. Sober's Western Lodge.

Lady Gosford's 'West Hill Lodge',
where Waitrose stands today.
Detail of the previous illustration.

12

More Recent Developments

The purpose of this book is to look at the original building and development of the area, and this process was more or less finished by the 1870s. The social history of its established population, and, for example, its experiences through two wars are another, presently unwritten story. However, some twentieth century events are a clear continuation of the building and developmental process, and so should be mentioned. They include the buying policy of the Children's Hospital, and the rebuilding of Clifton Mews.

During the late 1930s the Royal Alexandra Hospital for Sick Children became an important buyer of property at the top of the Hill. At that time Percy Spooner was the hospital secretary, and in the hospital archives there are various letters to and from Mr. Spooner regarding the numerous hospital properties. On September 8th 1937 the hospital purchased numbers 5, 6 & 7 Powis Villas, together with 23 and 23a Clifton Hill. All these properties were purchased for £5,300 from Mr. F.J. Wellman, who lived at 2 Powis Villas. On the same date the hospital also purchased land referred to as 21a Clifton Hill for £275.

Bearing in mind that throughout this study John Yearsley's house, Grove Villa, has been referred to as 23, these numbers of 21a, 23a and 23 Clifton Hill in the hospital records need an explanation. In October 1937 Mr. A.L. Gates wrote to his new landlord, Spooner, at the hospital, regarding the property known as 23 Clifton Hill, asking if they would grant him a more permanent lease – he suggested a three year agreement. In June 1938 he wrote again with the same request, noting the fact that he had been renting the premises, number 23, for 15 years prior to the hospital being the landlord, and that he sub-let to a Mr. Eves 'who took over the business, petrol pump and sundry plant'. He asked again for a longer lease than the current six monthly agreement, as his own tenant 'could not be expected to run a business on such a short term lease'. Until recently his petrol pump could still be seen in the flint barn, where Mr. Eves ran his business – presumably servicing and motor repairs. So the flint barn was the building that took over the number 23, until just a few years before the hospital itself was offered for sale by informal tender. (The closing date for these bids was 30th June 2006). The eventual sale of the Children's Hospital site gave an unexpected boost to NHS finances for the replacement hospital in Kemp Town. Until the bid date in June the expectation was something over £3m. In the *Argus* of December 19th 2006 the headline read, 'Royal Alex building sold for £10 million'. It was purchased by the developer George Wimpey.

In a letter of October 1937, 23a Clifton Hill is referred to as a builder's yard, with a rent of £4 pa. The hospital records also have a memorandum of agreement which identifies the flint barn as number 23 at the even earlier date of September 1919. This 1919 agreement is between George Lewis Browne of London, the landlord, and Richard William Frost, a Brighton pork butcher of 15 Gardner Street, who rents 'all that coach-house and stable (but not including yard to west of same) known as 23 Clifton Hill'. This must have been the tenant immediately prior to A.L. Gates, who appears in the 1920 Directory as the motor engineer of that address. It seems unlikely that Mr. Frost carried on his butchers business from the barn: possibly he just kept his delivery vans there, which is why the premises was suitable for the later motor car business.

This early landlord, George Lewis Browne, could well have been the grandson of Joseph Browne, the first owner of 5 Powis Villas. Joseph Browne died on 24th December 1862 leaving a son, George Joseph, described in the will as a gentleman of Lindfield, and two daughters, Elisa Emily Sabin and Maria Louisa Watson. He left his wife, Maria, an estate of nearly £50,000 and requested in his will that he be buried at Kensal Green cemetery.

When built, number 5 had large gardens, including the barn, but since George Lewis was described as 'from London', maybe he just kept the house and rented most of his land, thereby being the owner who finally separated the barn from the house, in September 1919. Presumably it was at the same time that Browne also disposed of that part of his garden that extended down to Powis Grove.

As Yearsley's home address became settled at 4 Powis Villas, this movement of the number 23 Clifton Hill is fairly logical. Moving up the Hill from Grove Villa (the original number 23, on the south side) discounting Aberdeen Lodge on the corner which is 5 Powis Villas, the next available building to take over the spare number 23 is the flint barn. The yard to the west (23a) has been used as the hospital staff car park. The property known as 21a Clifton Hill seems to refer to the back end of the rear garden of house 21, which portion of land now has a hospital out-building on it. In the 1931 Directory this address was already occupied by H. Wymark, upholsterer and Frederick Snell, a bootmaker, so presumably the hospital was not responsible for what appears to be the partitioning of the garden of number 21.

So in the 1930s F.J. Wellman was a considerable property owner in Powis Villas, living at number 2 and owning numbers 5, 6 and 7. When the hospital purchased these three houses, with a yard and a flint barn, they obviously took on tenants, as with Gates in the barn, and as soon as possible they put them on short agreements. A letter to Spooner from Mrs. Lewis of 6 Powis Villas also acknowledges six months notice, the same short lease Gates was arguing against, running from 3rd June 1939 'as you say you will require the premises'. The message from 5 Powis Villas is a little sadder. In a letter from that address, the tenant, Harold Bacon, mentions his attempt to use the property as a guest house, but the idea had failed and he 'lost every penny' – 'we shall not be able to carry on' renting the house. He offered to sell to the hospital the greenhouse, summer-house, coal-shed and garage he had built in the garden, which presumably has access through 23a. It was the hospital's original intention to redevelop all this land in Powis Villas, but the outbreak of war in 1939 put an end to these plans, so thankfully the houses and flint barn are still with us.

Moving on from medicine to education, apart from the early Church Hill school for the Workhouse children, and the Temple becoming an educational establishment by 1828, fee paying schools flourished so effectively in Brighton during the mid-nineteenth century that it was sometimes referred to as 'School Town', and our area certainly played its part. This growth of small schools was a direct result of the development of the town's middle classes. In the 1856 Directory Powis Square had seven schools, among them three ladies' and one gentlemen's boarding school and two preparatory schools for boys. There were two schools in Clifton Road, and one each in Clifton Terrace, Powis Grove, Clifton Place and Victoria Road.

A few years earlier, in 1852, there were 15 boarding schools for gentlemen and 21 boarding schools for young ladies listed in total, with the great majority being in Montpelier Road and Crescent. Interestingly, there was only one day school, run by Mrs. Davy at 39 Montpelier Street. With free compulsory elementary education by 1891, followed by the Education Act of 1902, few of these schools survived into the 20th century, but later on the area did have another school for boys and girls at 9 Powis Villas, that was run by the three Fuggles sisters. The two eldest ran the school, and the youngest sister ran their home, which was the house that was converted from the Clifton Arms public house, on the corner of Vine Place. It is not known when it was started, and it was apparently for girls only in the 1920s, but a male ex-pupil reports that it closed down in about 1954.

On the other side of the road from the Clifton Arms was the premises opened by the two Horton Stephens brothers as a lending library and stationers in about 1890, which business later evolved into a printers and survived into the 1990s.

On their early shop front they advertised themselves as 'Bookbinders and Letterpress, Lithographic and Copper Plate printers'.

Back down the Hill to the Mews again, a Brighton resident, the late Doris Roelich, remembers that (Harry?) Stapleton and his sons ran a haulage and transport business from Clifton Mews. By about 1930, when Doris shared rooms with one of the Stapleton daughters at 18 Hamilton Road, it was the sons of the family who were running the firm. The 1931 Directory adds some detail to this. A. Stapleton & Sons are listed as running their business from 15 Clifton Hill, and Frank Burn, furniture remover, is 12 and 14 Clifton Hill, number 12 being the house in the Mews immediately behind 11 Clifton Hill and 14 is the postal number of the Mews itself. Presumably Burn rented space in the Mews to Stapleton, and a third business in the area in 1931 was George Martin, a canine surgeon.

Moving to more modern times, an article from the local paper of 12th Sept. 1973 reports residents' alarm when the furniture dealer and owner of the Mews, David Hawkins, sent in workmen to demolish the house that was 15 Clifton Hill. As with Stapletons in the 1930s, number 15 still seemed to be associated with the business in the Mews. Apparently Mr. Hawkins' intention was to widen the eastern exit from the Mews for his furniture vans. As owner of the house, his demolition work was not illegal, but the immediate reaction of the borough surveyor, Noel Patterson, and the planning committee, was to put preservation orders on other houses on that side of the road. Local authorities are able to control the demise of unlisted buildings if their demolition would destroy the character or appearance of any part of a conservation area. The preserved houses in Clifton Hill are nos. 8 to 11, 13, and 16 to 22.

There were some ten years between the demolition of 15 Clifton Hill in September 1973 and the start of the redevelopment of the modern Clifton Mews. It is not clear whether David Hawkins was still involved with the Mews in the early 1980s, but he is not mentioned in a local *Gazette & Herald* article that discusses the proposed development. The date of the article is 1983 and Victor Gunn is identified as the proposer of the development scheme to build seven three-storey office blocks. Gunn had run a wholesale antiques business in the Mews for nearly eight years, but was moving to a new industrial site in Brighton. Gunn took over the premises from Hawkins, and the article gives us a good deal of information. At this time the houses 10 and 11 Clifton Hill had recently been restored by the Sussex Heritage Trust, but were still on the market. Number 11 was eventually purchased by Mr. & Mrs. Kandilal Doshi after they had moved down from Harringay, London, to take over the local post office. Mr. & Mrs. Doshi had previously escaped from Idi Amin's Uganda.

Apart from the offices, plans were also put forward to rebuild number 15, to renovate number 13 and then to rebuild the now derelict house number 12 (off the street in the Mews behind number 11) into three flats. This house, number 12, does not appear in the 1839 Leppard advertisement, and a reasonable guess is that it was built as the new residence for whichever tradesman was in the Mews when house number 13 was so radically changed to suit the fashionable nature of the newly developing Clifton Hill.

With number 12 being directly behind number 11, the latter number never had a back garden or back door. The present back wall of number 11 is made up of the chimney breast of the old number 12, and the original roof line of number 12 can still be seen just under the stacks, with the roof of the new flats starting several feet below it. The local architects, Briault and Smith, drew up the new Mews' plans.

The architect's drawing for the five office buildings in Clifton Mews.
The brick column far right is the side wall of the private house,
14 Clifton Hill, the front door of which faces these offices.

Gunn's plans were modified, and in the end his name did not figure as one of the developers. The demolished house 15 was rebuilt and joined to number 13 with a flying freehold, number 13 was renovated while the derelict number 12 (in the Mews itself and on the western edge) was demolished and the three modern flats were built. The planned number of offices was reduced from seven to five, and these were built at the farthest end of the area, away from the backs of the houses on Clifton Hill. The last two offices in the original plan were to be in the centre of the Mews, immediately behind house 13, but permission was refused and in their place the only detached residence inside the Mews, 14 Clifton Hill, was built.

This house, which has the address 14 Clifton Hill, Clifton Mews, was the first property to be occupied, in January 1986, and it holds an interesting place in the architectural development of central Brighton. Although built in 1985, to date it is still the only modern detached house ever to have been built in a Brighton conservation area, the builders inadvertently carrying on Mr. Yearsley's nineteenth century tradition of the detached homes of Powis Villas. The developers of the Mews were Old Temple Developments Ltd., a subsidiary of Sheraton Securities International plc, working in conjunction with the long established local builders, Rice & Sons Limited. The residential parts of the Mews were sold in reasonable time, but the offices, officially opened to view during the week of October 14th 1985, proved more difficult to sell or let. Rice & Sons had become financially involved with this development, and the delay on the return of their investment was instrumental in this old Sussex firm sadly going out of business in 1986.

The story now makes the connection with the post office, through Mr. & Mrs. Doshi mentioned earlier. In 1978 the original post office, now Headroom in Victoria Road, was owned by Mr. Sinhat, but it had been closed down by the head postmaster due to irregularities, and was on the market. In April that year Mr. Doshi agreed to buy the property leasehold, on condition that he was acceptable to the GPO and that the office would be re-opened. The vendor then changed his mind about selling, so Mr. Doshi agreed with the GPO to try to find another premises to buy. This he finally did, moving in on May 7th 1979. The new post office was now at 35 Clifton Hill, and Mr. & Mrs. Doshi first lived in the flat above, which was numbered 36. This is why it was called 'Victoria Road Post Office', even though it was in Clifton Hill.

Mr. Doshi's most frequent customer, with many letters and packages going to America, was Victor Gunn, from the Mews. Mr. Doshi remembers frequently collecting forms and post from Gunn's secretary, whose office was in the Mews house, number 12, described in the 1983 article as derelict. It was during 1983 that Gunn's business moved out of the Mews, from which time the area was unoccupied. In July 1985 the Doshi family purchased 11 Clifton Hill – the house to the left of the Mews' entrance – from the Sussex Heritage Trust. It had been on the market for several years and Mr. Doshi's correspondence shows that in 1972 this house had been owned by Leslie Robert Hartfield, who that year sold it to Frederick Mottershead.

Within a month or two of the Doshi family moving in, the peace of their new home, away from their work at the post office, was shattered, as Rice & Sons began building the modern development of Clifton Mews. This development of the Mews' land was the final chapter in its long and varied history. By 1839 its first business occupant on this piece of downland was Mrs. Watts' laundry service, with open fields behind her house. It then changed hands to Mr. Thomas the dairyman, then James Killner the wheelwright and on to J. Taylor, the post master and livery stables, serving the Crescent Inn. Later the removal and haulage business gave way to the antique furniture trade, and now, finally it is an office development, first taken by the Crown Prosecution Service until they vacated the offices in 2002.

The Mews, now Clifton Mews, is the oldest surviving site on the road to Blatchington, the business and home address for Mrs. Watts of Lone Cottage before the residential development of Church Hill – West Side had begun. As it was in 1839, so once again in the 21st century it is the most modern business site on Church Hill – West Side.

NOTES TO THE TEXT

Note 1.
The Baring family:
    Sir Francis Baring 1st Bt. (1740-1810)
    His elder son - Thomas (1772-1848) succeeded as 2nd Bt. in 1810.
    Sir Francis's second son - Alexander, later 1st Lord Ashburton (1774-1848).
    Sir Francis's brother was John Baring, the co-founders in 1770 of what was regarded as
    the first merchant bank in Europe.
    Remembering the collapse of Barings, courtesy of Mr. Leeson, in the mid 1990s, parts of this company's financial history make interesting reading. In 1885, when Sir Francis Baring was raised to the peerage as Baron Revelstoke, the bank stood at the height of its prosperity. In the following years Barings became deeply involved in loans and interest guarantees to the Argentine, and towards the end of 1890 it became known that the bank was about to suspend all payments, with liabilities of £21m. Disaster was only averted by the prompt action of the Bank of England which, with other UK banks, took over the liabilities and reorganised Baring Brothers with fresh capital of £1m. (Britannica 1957)

Note 2.
George Aitchison (1926) writes about the origins of the Wick Estate.
Quote from p64: 'There is plenty of evidence that . . . . Wick was a separate hamlet, between Brighton and Hove. The etymologists will tell us that "Wick" and "Vik" are the same word. Every boy knows that Vikings are the Vik-ings, the sons of the creek. When the Danes were in Sussex, Wick was on the banks of a creek.'

Note 3.
William Hallett died at 142 Marine Parade on 3rd April 1862. His first wife, Mary Ann had pre-deceased him, and he left two sons by her, William Henry and Frederick Francis. By an indenture on 22nd May 1858 he had conveyed his half share in the Steam Brewery of Lewes to William Henry, the business partner owning the other half being Henry Abbey. In the will, dated 13th March 1862, he left £14,000, of which £400 went to his second wife, Harriett Rebecca, with whom he had a third son, John. The will goes on to mention a range of Sussex properties that he owned. These included a house in Church Street, Beeding, a blacksmith's shop in Hereford Street, Brighton, Warren Farm in Rottingdean parish and Black Rock Farm (also called Manor Farm) in Brighton parish. These two farms, totalling 300 acres, were leasehold properties left to his eldest son but farmed and sub-leased by Frederick Francis. Further leasehold properties included two inns in Uckfield, the King's Head and the Bell, and the White Hart at Buxted. He also owned a brewery at Uckfield, which was left to the eldest son in trust for the youngest, John, until he was 21. There was also a half-share in the freehold of the War Bill Inn at Warbleton.

Note 4.
William Heaves Smithers' father was also named William Heaves, and our Brighton based W.H.S. junior was the eldest son of ten children. The father, Smithers senior (1781–1852) emigrated to Western Australia in 1829 and received a 2,500 acre grant, which land he named Albion Town. He was an hotelier and had ambitious plans for the land, but because

of changes to the government's timetable for development, he had to off sell off parcels of the grant for farmers to develop. His wife, Susannah, who died in 1839, is buried on a part of this land surrounding Haddrill House, in Swan District, which was a colony of the first European settlers. Two weeks after Susannah's death Smithers senior surrendered most of his undeveloped land grant back to the government, and in fact he died back in England. Two other brothers of William Heaves junior (1807–1892), James and George, settled in Cape Town SA in the 1830s. (Internet sites accessed 2007 – Genealogy.com and Register of Heritage Places).

Note 5.
G.E.Payne, in the booklet on Hove Parish Church, writes, 'Hove remained a poor village, and its church diminished from the flourishing beginnings in the twelfth century, when St. Andrew's was built, to its use as a storehouse in the eighteenth century, when services were held about every six weeks and, more often than not, out of doors, since the building was too decrepit and too full of rubbish and contraband merchandise to be used. In 1836 the church was indifferently restored to its present appearance.'

Note 6.
F. Harrison and J.S.North (1937), in their publication *Old Brighton, Old Preston, Old Hove*, write about this convent dedicated to St. Bartholomew:
    'The Priory of St. Bartholomew – first record of it is c1185 . . . and as there is no mention of it in the confirmation of the gift of the church of Brighton by Henry 1, there is reason for believing that it was not built until after 1120. When the chapel of St. Bartholomew was destroyed, the Prior's Lodge was spared and became, after the Reformation, the residence of the vicar of Brighton until 1790, when it was demolished. The then vicar, Rev. T. Hudson, built a new vicarage a few yards to the north, on the corner of Nile Street. This house was sold in 1834, and the third vicarage was built in Montpelier Road by George Cheesman 1834/35, which ended the glorious isolation that Kemp's Temple had hitherto enjoyed.' The authors then mention that now (1937) it is an annexe of the High School: 'In 1836 this vicarage was acquired by a group of businessmen, and opened as a commercial school for the middle-classes – later moving to 6 Ship Street.'

Note 7.
The dealings over the triangle of land bounded by Clifton Hill, Dyke Road and Clifton Road are not easy to follow, and are further complicated by the separate history of the south-eastern tip that became the site of the Children's Hospital. At the time of publication, the time-line seems to be as follows:
By 1821 Mr. Heard was leasing the tip of the larger triangle of land from T.R.Kemp. Presumably Heard built himself a small business premises from which he ran a soap manufacturing business, and a candle-making business.
In 1822 Heard's business failed and the Rev. Airey took over the lease for this piece of land, together with Heard's building, and opened a school for the workhouse children.
In 1823 Airey purchased the school house estate from Kemp.
In 1832 Kemp mortgaged the remainder of the larger triangle of land to Budgen. Obviously this did not include the school house site.
At a date not yet established Airey sold the school house estate to the Rev. Butler.
In 1843 Budgen's executors called in the mortgage and sold the larger triangle of land to

Thomas Wisden. Wisden sold on part to the Rev. Butler, who already owned the school house, and Butler sold on part of his purchase to William Watts.

At a date not yet established Butler sold the school house to the Rev. Pugh.

In 1870 Pugh sold the school house estate to the governing body of the Children's Hospital, who then moved up to Church Hill from their two converted houses on Western Road.

Note 8.

Henry Phillips of Brighton (1779–1840) was born in Henfield, and after a time spent in Brighton he moved to Bayswater, London, in 1815, to open an academy for young gentlemen. He returned to Brighton in 1823, where his wife also ran an academy for young ladies. Phillips gave up running schools and concentrated on lecturing in botany. He published many important early nineteenth century books on the subject, including *A History of Cultivated Vegetables* in 1822.

Note 9.

The purpose behind the typical nineteenth century topographical or architectural drawing or painting of a town like Brighton was very different from the development of the earlier Georgian print market in England. Original paintings by the fine eighteenth century English artists were only occasionally seen at exhibitions or on visits to wealthy homes, so their mezzotint engravings communicated the artists' work throughout the UK, and to eager markets around Europe. By contrast, many of the original drawings behind the copper plate and steel engravings of Brighton were executed purely for the purpose of print making for the local and visitors' market, with many being lost or discarded after the engraving process was complete.

Note 10.

In an unpublished manuscript 'The Palmers of Montpelier Road' (private collection) Eric Underwood quotes a letter of March 14th 1837 from Edmund Palmer to his mother. Edmund, son of the famous John Palmer of Bath, was a pupil at the Rev Fennell's academy at the Temple, he was just approaching his twelfth birthday, and he writes: 'In my studies I am reading the fourteenth section of Sallust and the third Aeneid of Virgil; in Greek I am reading the first Delectus and the Testament, and in grammar I am at anomalous verbs. In English I learn Geography, History and Johnson's Dictionary and in French I am reading Tresor and Gil Blas. I have nearly finished the map of southern Greece'. He then goes on to bemoan the fact that they have not been to the Chain Pier for a fortnight or three weeks.

BIBLIOGRAPHY

Aitchison, George. 'Unknown Brighton'
    John Lane The Bodley Head Ltd., London 1926.

Andrews, M. & Crisfield. M. 'Brighton & Hove'
    Frances Lincoln Ltd. 2006.

Beavis, J. 'The Brighton Races'.
    J. Beavis 2003.

Beevers, David. MA.   'St. Michael and All Angels Church, Brighton',
    A History and Guide.
    St. Michael & All Angels PCC., 1993.

Beevers, David. MA. 'Brighton Revealed – Through Artists' Eyes c1760–c1960'
    Royal Pavilion, Art Gallery and Museums, Brighton 1995.

Belton, R.H.   'William Vine – a Sussex Miller'
    Article in the Sussex County Magazine.

Berry, Sue. 'Georgian Brighton'
    Phillimore & Co. Ltd 2005.

Beswick, M. 'Brickmaking in Sussex'
    Middleton Press, 1993

Bishop, J.G. 'A Peep into the Past: Brighton in The Olden Times'.
    No publication line, but first published in 1880 and reprinted 1892.
    Bishop is described as Printer, 'Herald' Office, Brighton.

Boddie, Rob – Librarian of Sussex CCC.
    The Sussex Cricket Club library was started in 1953 and now has over 1,000 books on
    cricket.

Bramwell, F. 'The Windmills of Brighton'
    Article in The Brighton Herald, 6-13 August 1938.

Brighton & Hove Libraries – The Times on line – Digital Archive 1785 – 1985. accessed
    2006.

Brodribb, Gerald. The Sussex CCC Handbook. 1951.

Brown, Val. 'Women's Hospitals in Brighton & Hove'.
    The Hastings Press 2006.

Carder, Tim. 'Encyclopaedia of Brighton'.
   East Sussex County Library 1990.

cmpcanews9.
   The Clifton Montpelier Powis Community Association newsletter, September 2007 –
   'The Powis Square History Project', page 14.

Dale, Antony. 'Fashionable Brighton 1820–1860'.
   Country Life 1947, and Oriel Press 1967

Dale, Antony. 'About Brighton'
   The Regency Society of Brighton & Hove, 1951.

Dale, Antony. 'The History & Architecture of Brighton'.
   S.R. Publishers. Second edition 1972.

Dale, Antony. 'Brighton Town and Brighton People'
   Phillimore & Co. Ltd.1976.

Dawes, H.T. 'The Windmills and Millers of Brighton'.
   Lewis Cohen Urban Studies in conjunction with The Sussex Industrial Archaeology
   Society. Undated.

d'Enno, Douglas. 'From Workhouse to Warren Farm'
   Article in the *Argus*, July 24th 2004.

d'Enno, Douglas. 'Brighton Crime and Vice 1800 – 2000'
   Wharncliffe Books 2007.

Dinkel, John. 'The Royal Pavilion, Brighton'.
   Philip Watson, 1993.

Doyne-Ditmus, Julia. 'Hampton Villa & its Residents – A Case Study in Local History'
   Private manuscript – April 2000.

East Sussex Record Office.
   AMS 6382, 6343, 6345, DB/B66/58, DB/B73/72.

Erredge, J.A. 'History of Brighthelmston'.
   Brighton 1862. Printed by E. Lewis, North Street.

Erredge, J.A. 'History of Brighthelmston', with a New Introduction by John Farrant.
   Brambletye Books 2005.

Farrant, John & Sue – editors. 'Aspects of Brighton 1650–1800'.
   University of Sussex Centre for Continuing Education 1978.

Finch, M.L. 'Windmills at Work in East Sussex'.
    SB Publications 2004.

Fines, Ken. 'A History of Brighton & Hove'.
    Phillimore & Co. 2004

Fleet, W & C. 'An Illustrated Hand-Book of Brighton and its Environs'.
    Fleet 1847.

Flower, R. 'The Old Ship – A Prospect of Brighton'.
    Croom Helm 1986.

Folthorp, R. General Directory for Brighton, Hove and Cliftonville,
    1848, 1850, 1861 and 1862.

Ford, John and Jill. 'Images of Brighton'.
    Saint Helena Press, 1981.

Ford, John. 'Coachmaker – The Life and Times of Philip Godsal'.
    Quiller Press 2005.

Gilbert, E.W. 'Brighton, Old Ocean's Bauble'.
    Methuen, 1954.

Grant, Roy 'mybrightonandhove' website accessed 2006.

Gray, J.S. – notes on the Powis District of Brighton, No.25.
    Private manuscript by J.S.Gray.

Harrison, F. 'The Story of Brighton, Hove and Neighbourhood'.
    Southern Publishing Co. 1931.

Harrison, F. & North. J.S. 'Old Brighton, Old Preston, Old Hove'.
    Flare Books 1937.

Hitchin-Kemp, Fred. 'The Kemp and Kempe Families of Great Britain and Her Colonies'
    The Leadenhall Press – 1902.

Horlock, Chris. 'The Neat and Nippy Guide to Brighton's History'
    S B Publications 2005.

Martin, Alderman Henry. 'The History of Brighton and Environs'.
    John Beal, East Street, 1871.

Middleton, Judy 'A History of Hove'
    Phillimore 1979.

Moore, Joy S. 'Three Brighton Streets', a study of the building and first occupation of Victoria Street, Montpelier Street and Montpelier Villas, between 1841 and 1851.
    Unpublished manuscript, c1970 Brighton History Centre – ref SB9 MOO.

Musgrave, Clifford. 'Life in Brighton'.
    Rochester Press 1981

Richardson, John 'The Local Historian's Encyclopedia'.
    Historical Publications 2003.

Robertson's Brighton & Hove.
Written and compiled by H. Mackinnon Walbrook.
Brighton Society and Guardian Press Ltd. Undated, but c1899.

Robinson, L.J. 'The Lanes of Brighton'.
    Southern Publishing Company 1967.

Robson, Professor David and Macdonald. Ken. 'A Guide to the Buildings of Brighton'.
    McMillan Martin Ltd. Undated but produced in 1987 and never put on general sale.
    Robson and Macdonald acted as editors to the work of Clive Atkinson, David Matthews,
    Andrew Savile, Robert Tunna and Tim Weighill, final year students in The School of
    Architecture and Interior Design of Brighton Polytechnic.

Ryman, E. & Mead. G. 'Glimpses of Old Brighton'.
    Dyke Publications 1994.

Salzman, L.F. Editor of 'The Victoria History of the County of Sussex'
    Oxford University Press, 1940.

Saunders, W. & Son. 'The Strangers' Guide in Brighton'. 1837 and 1855.

Sawyer, F.E. 'Land Division and Tenure in Brighton and the Neighbourhood'.
    Spottiswoode & Co. 1881.

Simmons, H.E.S. The principle source of all books on C19th windmills in Sussex and
    beyond. Mr. Simmons collected a great deal of information during a period of over forty
    years, but his work was never published.

Sitwell, O. & Barton, M. 'Brighton'.
    Faber & Faber 4th edition, 1949.

Spector, David. 'Victorian Jewry 1837 – 1901 Brighton'
    Unpublished manuscript, Brighton History Centre, ref. BRI 942.2

Squire, H.F. and A.P. 'Pre-Victorian Sussex Cricket'
    Printed by The Ditchling Press 1951.

Taylor, W.J. The Original Brighton & Hove Directory for 1854.

The Times on line. Accessed 2006/7

Underwood, E.   'Brighton'.
    B.T.Batsford, London 1978.

Wagner, A. & Dale, A.   'The Wagners of Brighton'.
    Phillimore 1983.

Wales, T. 'Brighton and Hove' – the Archive Photographs series.
    Chalford Publishing Company 1997.

Wallis's Royal Edition 'Brighton As It Is' 1836.

INDEX